COURTNEY

Master Oarsman — Champion Coach

Other books by Margaret K. Look

At Home On The Workhouse Farm

At Home In Pittsburgh

Cover Illustration By
Linda Cook DeVona

COURTNEY

Master Oarsman — Champion Coach

by

Margaret K. Look

Margaret K. Look

Empire State Books
Interlaken, New York
1989

Library of Congress Cataloging-in-Publication

Look, Margaret K. (Margaret Kincaid)
Courtney : master oarsman, champion coach / by Margaret K. Look.
p. cm.
Includes bibliographical references.
1. Courtney, Charles Edward, 1849–1920. 2. Rowers—United States—Biography. 3. Rowing—United States—Coaches—Biography. 4. Cornell University—Rowing. I. Title.
ISBN: 1-55787-044-6 (pbk)
GV790.92.C68L66 1989
797.1'23'092—dc20 [B] 89–36852 CIP

Manufactured in the United States of America
ISBN: 1-55787-044-6

A *quality* publication of
Heart of the Lakes Publishing
Interlaken, New York 14847

Dedicated

to

All the men and women
who have rowed for Cornell.

CONTENTS

FOREWORD

by John Ferriss

Rowing's roots go back 2000 years in transportation and warfare; London's ferrymen raced for a coat 270 years ago; schools, colleges, and clubs raced during the last 150 years. Popular paintings by Thomas Eakins give some clue that in the late 1800s, before basketball was invented, rowing and sculling were ardently followed by media and spectators. But much of those times are a mystery to modern rowers. Old boathouses, old equipment, trophies, banners, and pictures all help our imagination play with what it might have been like to row 100 years ago. Now Margaret Look gives us an opportunity to learn about one man, Charles Courtney sculling one hundred and twenty years ago, and some of the legendary events—promoters, gambling, poisoning, boats sawed in half—that were instrumental in shaping our rowing world.

In Ithaca the memory of Charles Courtney is faint. His name along with R. Harrison "Stork" Sanford identify the Cornell rowing endowment fund, and his picture occupies prominent locations at both the boathouse and indoor training facility on campus. Pictures from his era and a shell he rowed also are displayed on the walls of Teagle Hall; but what he did, who he was, and how he lived are not widely known. The original Cornell boathouse where Courtney coached, damaged by fire in 1956, was replaced by the John L. Collyer Boathouse in 1957. Fortunately the circa 1895 boathouse of Cascadilla school, where Courtney coached in 1895 and 1896, has been preserved by the City of Ithaca and is now used by the Cascadilla Boat Club.

The first year I was in Ithaca a former Dean of the College of Agriculture and Life Science, Ted Baldwin, told me a few Courtney stories from his rowing days, 1915 to 1919. Those nearly forgotten stories helped fuel my imagination of the "Old Man," but created a different personality from that presented by C. V. P. Young in *Courtney and Cornell Rowing*. Exploring the basement of Teagle Hall a few years ago I found a trunk of "junk" that turned out to be priceless historic artifacts. With a newspaper reporter's inquisitiveness Margaret Look has searched through the letters, daily logs, and notes from that trunk; she also went back to newspaper reports of 120 years ago, and talked to or corresponded with people who rowed on some of Courtney's crews. Having time as her ally she was able to explore all sides of the man, his life, and his impact on the University.

One of my favorite stories from Courtney's logs was entered the day after he first used a launch with an internal combustion engine. Originally his coaching launch was steam powered. During the spring, after the ice was gone, air temperatures could still dip down into the twenties, so someone would have to stay up all night putting fuel into the fire under the boiler to keep it from freezing. Everyone was delighted to have a new, modern, gasoline powered launch, but on the first day in use it broke down out on the lake, and the crews were sent back with instructions to have the boatman come tow them in with the old, dependable, steam engine launch.

For the last twenty years one of the complex issues facing American rowing has been the distinction between amateurism and professionalism. The roots of an ardent philosophy of amateurism go back to Courtney's time and the problems that were associated with professional sculling. Creation of the National Association of Amateur Oarsmen, now the United States Rowing Association, was based in the need to free amateur rowers from the powerfully negative reputation associated with professionals. Today's rowers have been both proud of and frustrated by the strict amateur standards of our sport. As rowing moves into the gray area between the two extremes, standards of amateurism are being loosened with broken time payments, advertising endorsements, and training subsidies, it will be helpful to gain historic perspective on the basis for our current amateur code.

With the recent publication of several books presenting a broad picture of rowing traditions and practice it is very satisfying to also be able to read about one man and a special period in American rowing. You will be as amazed as I was to learn of the scheming and attempted manipulation common in professional rowing. Coming to Cornell allowed Courtney to stay with his beloved sport, avoid corruption, and positively influence many individual students as well as an entire university.

Teagle Hall
Cornell University
May 1989

ACKNOWLEDGEMENTS

I extend special thanks to the following for their assistance in preparing this book: Thomas Eldred, Marjorie Gibbs, John Ferriss, Thomas Mendenhall, Norma Bilak, Gould P. Colman and the staff of the Department of Manuscripts and University Archives, Cornell University. And I thank my family and friends for listening patiently for many years to my tales about Charles Courtney.

Photo credits as *Cornell Archives* are from the Courtney collection, boxes 40/1/924 and 40/1/142, and reproduced courtesy of the Department of Manuscripts and University Archives, Cornell University Library, Ithaca, NY 14853–5301.

PROLOGUE

In the fall of 1933, when I first arrived on the Cornell University campus, people still talked about "Pop" Courtney, although he had been dead for thirteen years. Charles Edward Courtney had been the rowing coach who trained winning crews at Cornell for more than three decades.

There seemed to be a Courtney mystique—a reverence for the man who in his youth had been a champion oarsman and a skilled carpenter and then, despite his lack of formal education, had become a leading trainer of young men. What was it about this man that enabled him to have such a profound influence on hundreds of young men, and to establish a reputation that endures today? I pondered this question then, as I do today.

My interest in Courtney has continued during the many years since I learned to row under the tutelage of women coaches whom he had taught. This interest was increased by research for a magazine article about his aborted race as the champion American single sculler against the leading Canadian, Edward Hanlan, when Courtney's boat was sawed in two the night before the race. Since then I have continued to learn about this man, fondly called "Pop" Courtney or "The Old Man" by hundreds of Cornellians. Some people say he was called "Pop" Courtney only when he was absent, but the fact remains that hundreds of Cornellians respected his ability and judgment and thought of him with the affection that accompanies the nickname "Pop."

Courtney was called a master oarsman and champion coach, thus summing up his two careers. When a young man in his twenties, he rowed eighty-eight races as an amateur single sculler and never lost one. After becoming a professional oarsman in 1877, he rowed forty-six races and lost seven. A measure of Courtney's coaching ability is found in a statement made by the men in the Class of 1912 when they met to honor him. They said, "In his own field he is without peer. He understands the science of rowing, both practical and theoretical, he knows much about boat building and the art of riggers, but above all, he knows men and how to bring out the best that is in them."

The book *Courtney And Cornell Rowing,* by Charles Van Patten Young, thoroughly covers Courtney's coaching career. Therefore, in this book I shall describe just a few highlights of his coaching days. The emphasis will be on Courtney the man, starting with his youth, through his rowing career as an amateur and professional oarsman in the heyday of the sport, and continuing with episodes that illustrate his abilities as a coach.

E. B. White wrote in the *Cornell Daily Sun:* "Many years may pass, and still Cornellians will look back into the shadowy past and recall the bluff, old figure standing in his launch bellowing commands across the water to a rhythmic crew. His memory will live on to haunt the lake and valley and the story of his genius will be handed down to inspire the crews that are to come."

The mystique may not be explained in these pages, but I trust the reader will enjoy meeting this unusual man, who in his later years was called "the grand old man of rowing."

CHAPTER 1

THE EARLY YEARS

His place of birth, his inherited physical characteristics and his family's circumstances probably were the major factors that determined the career and success of Charles Courtney. Also significant were the circumstances and customs of the era in which he lived.

Born in the village of Union Springs on the northeastern shore of Cayuga Lake in New York State, he grew up near the water, learning to swim and handle boats early in life. As a child in a large family left fatherless when he was quite young, he learned the carpentry trade to make a living and used this skill in his long experience with rowing. During his lifetime, from his birth in 1849 until his death in 1920, the United States experienced rapid growth and many changes. Railroads, steamboats and the telegraph greatly enhanced transportation and communication. An affluent populace had time for sporting events, either as participants or spectators. Rowing was one of the sports that grew and attracted wide attention and support in this era. Courtney, first as a champion oarsman and then as a master coach, was a major participant.

Both his parents, James Thomas Courtney and Catherine Coburn, were born in Ireland, came to America when young and lived in Salem, Massachusetts where James was a landscape gardener. After their marriage in 1840, they moved to Union Springs at the request of George Howland who hired Courtney to develop the gardens for the houses he had built for his son and daughter.

At the time, the Courtneys had two children, Thomas and Alice. Later they had seven more children, two of whom died in infancy. Of the surviving seven children, Charles, born on

November 13, 1849, was the next to the youngest. He was six years old when his father died in 1855.

Charlie, as he was called, remembered his father as a big, burly, good-natured man with a deep voice, who would carry him down the road on his back or romp with him and his older brothers after the evening meal had been eaten and the dishes put away in the large, old-fashioned cupboard, the most prominent piece of furniture in the house.

The family was Roman Catholic. When St. Michael's Parish was established in the village, the first services were held in the Courtney home.

Charlie's mother had memories of her son as a toddler that may have indicated his future. She used to say that he never crept like most babies. He used to sit up very straight on the floor, put his hands to his sides and go twice as far as he could have crawled. "His clothing was always in a deplorable condition until I found a way to protect it. I took an old oil-skin coat, like fishermen wear, and made slip-overs for him. Then he could play his game. I think even as a baby he would measure the distance he wished to slide, because he always reached the spot aimed at, then would sit still and look back over his shoulder to see if he had made it," she said.

Charles Courtney was born in a house that originally stood on the foundation where the library in Union Springs now stands. The library building was formerly used as a Quaker Meetinghouse. When he grew up he built his own house on land in this same square of property, a stone's throw, as he said, from Cayuga Lake.

Courtney remembered that as a boy he and his friends had fun peeking at the Quakers, through the door or through the window by climbing on the window ledge to look at the solemn-faced Friends at their meeting.

"From the time I was old enough to walk," Charlie said, "I was always around the water. I could swim at five or six years of age, as soon as I had strength enough, and I was always crazy to go into the skiffs."

On one memorable day he was the proudest boy in Union Springs. As usual he was hanging around the docks, when one of the boats that had just been completed would not slide off the ways. A workman caught up Charlie and tossed him aboard the new boat. With the additional weight she slid gracefully into the water. The men cheered and called little Charlie a hero.

Although James Courtney was a hard-working, frugal man, his widow and the large family of children were left in poor circumstance when he died. "We all had to hustle," Charlie said in later years.

At this time Union Springs was one of the most popular places in the state for pleasure boating and racing yachts. All during Charlie Courtney's youth and young manhood, there was great community interest in the boating on the lake, especially in the racing yachts. Communities along the shores of Cayuga and Seneca lakes sponsored their own yachts and kept up a lively competition for thirty years. Summer residents

Cornell Archives

The house in which Charles Courtney was born in Union Springs, New York is shown at right. It also is in the foreground of the picture, above.The house used to stand on the foundation where the library now stands on Main Street in Union Springs. The large building at right, rear, is the Spring Mills, called Howland Mills in Courtney's notes.

came to the lake from New York and other cities, helping to maintain the pleasure boating industry. Young boys who hung around the docks could earn a little money by grabbing a line or in some way helping a boatman.

Charlie Courtney's love of boats was an all year-affair. "I can well remember how I used to run away from school to help the boys put black lead on the bottom of the boats and polish 'em up. Each of us had his favorite, and when they were all ready to go forth to race we could at least stand on the dock and cheer for them," he said.

"I could row a boat when I was seven and go anywhere on the water, and we had races about every evening after school," Courtney told Professor Waterman Thomas Hewett, the author of *Cornell University—A History* (1905).

"When I was about twelve years old, I made up my mind that I could build a boat of my own. I got hold of some hemlock boards for the sides and a two-inch plank for the bottom, but, boy-like, cut the plank all around with an ax, canoe-shape, and tried to fit it inside of the boards, when I ought to have nailed the plank right on the boards and then trimmed enough off all around the outside."

"Of course, it was a poor job," Courtney continued. "I took yellow clay and plastered it into the crevices, but the water would force it off in no time, and then the boat went down like lead."

The boys, however, had fun racing in her. The conditions of the race were to see who could go around a stick about fifteen rods out in the lake and back again before the boat sank. "I don't remember anybody getting around that stick and back again before she went down," Courtney said. "No one ever won that race," he added.

When reminiscing about the racing with his young friends in other boats in those days, Courtney said he was strong and large for his age, which gave him an advantage. They had a method of rowing three in a boat, one in the middle and one on each side, and "if we did not have the right ones we would, of course, come in second."

Courtney, who was recognized as a better oarsman than

the average boy, had a different style of rowing. "I don't know how I happened to pick it up, but it was the style I always had and is the same that I am teaching these boys here at Cornell," he said in 1905.

Nellie Larmon Anthony, niece of Charlie and daughter of his sister Alice Larmon, wrote about some of his escapades in these early years in *Master Coach.* She says that one summer he found a deserted, tumbled down boathouse along the lake shore and appropriated it, bringing his fishing gear and tools there. Nearby was a small house where a man named Patsy lived. On a cold, fall morning, when Charlie was working at his boathouse, he felt the need for some heat and took a big piece of wood from the large pile by Patsy's house. He had just turned his back on the way to his place when Patsy called to him, "Help yerself, Charlie. Help yerself, me lad."

Startled and ashamed, Charlie said, "Oh, Patsy. I didn't know you were home. I wasn't going to steal the wood, but it is so cold and I want to work and I knew you would not care about one piece of wood." And he started to put it back.

"Charlie, me lad, take that wood. If you don't, I'll lick ye. Take it, and I'll help ye light ye're fire."

From this experience a lasting friendship developed between the boy and the man. In the summer, when Charlie rowed long miles on the lake, often in a boat he had made himself, and came back to his boathouse, it was Patsy who pulled in the boat, Patsy who laid the big, tired lad out on a straw tick and gave him a good rub, then watched while he slept, Mrs. Larmon wrote.

During the early years, two men figured prominently in Courtney's life and career. One of them was Captain John Carr

Captain John Carr of Union Springs, who taught Courtney how to sail.

Cornell Archives

who taught him how to sail a boat. Carr, a hunter, sailor and fisherman of considerable local fame, had grown up on the lake shore at Carr's Cove. When he thought Charlie could handle a sailboat satisfactorily, he would take the boy with him while he placed a large number of duck decoys in the lake. Then Carr would crawl into a floating battery or sink-box and tell Charlie to sail around and scare up the ducks.

Captain Carr and Charles Courtney remained friends for many years, the younger man learning much about boat building and handling from the captain.

The other man who influenced the life of young Charlie was Silas Ludlow. "I came to adopt the carpenter trade through Mr. Ludlow, who was building a boat, and nights after school I used to watch him and hold up the ends of the boards for him. Whenever he saw me he would say, 'There comes my carpenter.' "

Soon Ludlow was permitting Charlie to saw off the boards. One night Charlie said, "Uncle Silas, I can saw with one hand as well as with the other."

"Yes," replied Ludlow. "I can, too, and a little bit better."

In later years Courtney said he got his idea of learning carpentry from his experiences with Ludlow. After finishing at the high school, he was apprenticed to Ludlow, worked with Jerry Jaquith, another carpenter, and later with Emmet Anthony, an architect.

While he was still in school, Charlie made a boat that launched him on his rowing career. His friend, William Cozzens, who was a clerk in the post office, happened to see a magazine article describing a 1,000–mile trip by a Mr. McGregor through England, Scotland and Europe in a little boat, called a canoe, which was 24 inches wide, 9 inches deep and 16 feet long. It was named *Rob Roy.* The two young men decided to build just such a boat, even though they had no money, no lumber and little experience.

Their workroom was the basement of the post office. Their tools were a hacksaw, a hammer and a smooth plane. "How did we get the lumber?" Courtney reminisced years later. "Well,

Photo by the author

Howland millpond, as it looks today, was where Courtney launched his first boat, the *Rob Roy.*

the less said about that lumber the better; some of it we came by legitimately, and some of it we got boy-fashion."

They used the dimensions of the McGregor boat and built theirs with a red and white cedar deck. They propelled it with a double-bladed paddle. When the boat was finished, Courtney said, "It was a beauty!"

He gave much of the credit to his friend Cozzens, but all who saw Courtney's later work knew that he had done his share.

As they carried it through town to Howland's millpond, the bystanders shook their heads and said that, surely, the boys had built themselves a coffin. It was christened the *Rob Roy* after the McGregor boat, and was soon making circuits of the pond with all the boys and men taking turns with the double-bladed paddle. "That was the beginning of my boating and racing career," Courtney said.

In the late summer of 1868, the young men in Union

Springs read in a newspaper about a paper boat, narrow and long, that was going to be rowed in a race. Courtney and Cozzens were curious about the paper boat. They decided to try propelling their boat with oars. Having no money to buy the oars, they made them.

And just in time. Soon after the oars were finished, the news came that there was to be a yacht race and a single scull race at Aurora—on their own lake.

Captain James Angel, a veteran of the Civil War and later postmaster at Union Springs, urged Courtney to enter the sculling race. "What's a single scull race?" Courtney asked.

No one could answer him specifically because no one in Union Springs knew much about the wooden shell boats and the paper boats, sometimes called "needle boats," that were being used in rowing races. For about two decades Americans had been getting interested in rowing as a sport and adopting many of the boat styles and rowing regulations used by the British. Now, shortly after the Civil War, this interest would skyrocket to make rowing the leading national sport in the 1870s and early 1880s.

Captain Angel had told the people at Aurora that Charlie Courtney had built a little, narrow boat and he would try to persuade the young man to row. "They all got after me and were bound I should go," Courtney recalled. "I thought the *Rob Roy* was the smallest and nicest boat in the world, and finally consented to go," he added.

On the morning of the race, Courtney put his boat on the steamer and went to Aurora, where some of his friends met him, full of apprehension. "There're two men here with those shell boats! You never saw such looking things in your life; just so wide," one of Courtney's friends said, indicating with his hands a very short distance.

"I went over to the storehouse and saw those boats, looking like two bars of polished steel—12 inches wide and finished as beautifully as a piano body. 'Let's go cover up my boat,' I said," Courtney recalled.

Courtney's boat had been taken from the steamer and put on Captain Angel's sailboat. "She was quite a curiosity to the

Cornell Archives

Courtney is shown at Union Springs in 1868 in the first racing boat he ever owned. It was lapstreak, 19 inches wide, 25 feet long and was built at Geneva. On the shore are, from left, F. H. Hartman, N. S. Collins, N. C. Howland. Dr. Caulkins is in the distance. Charles Myers is on the boat in the rear. Courtney wrote this information on the back of the picture.

crowd—a boy's boat in every sense of the word. The New Yorkers went out and looked at her and poked each other in the ribs and winked. I was just as ashamed of her as I could be. Their shells weighed thirty pounds apiece; mine weighed nearly eighty," Courtney said.

Captain Angel went to Courtney and said, "Charlie, I want you to win that race. Go in, for I know that you can beat those chaps even if they have got better boats than you."

"He knew I was strong as a horse," Courtney reminisced.

The race was to begin about three o'clock over a three-mile course, one and a half miles out and one and a half back. Crowds gathered around the men from New York as they got into their slim, shell boats. The local people expressed disbelief that anyone could really sit in them, and here were big, husky men rowing away in these strange boats!

In later years, Courtney described his feelings that day to

Professor Hewett: "I don't suppose I shall ever be able to tell the feelings and sensations that came over me when I got into my boat, or the looks of pity on the faces of my friends who wanted to see me win, but didn't think I had the ghost of a show.

"W. H. Bogart of Aurora started the race, and when we were backed up to the line I knew that I was in a boat and I was out there and was going to try to beat somebody. If those shell boats were a surprise to all concerned, I may say that the race was a bigger one. I just literally ran away from those two oarsmen, right straight from the word 'Go'.

"Every inch I pulled harder, for I was afraid they might catch me in those boats. Never will I forget the expression on their faces as I shot away from them. They looked around at me, but never said a word. And when it was all over, it was found I had beaten them in the three miles by nearly half a mile. Time, thirty odd minutes—they just guessed it off. Of course, my opponents were no good as oarsmen, or I could never have beaten them, handicapped by a boat more than twice as heavy as theirs."

Courtney's friends cheered and cheered as their local man won by such a big margin. Bogart presented him the prize, a little silver cup, which the oarsman cherished more than all the awards he won later.

This race at Aurora in 1868 marked the beginning of an interest in rowing among the people at Union Springs, Courtney said. However, during the following summer, 1869, he did not row much.

He said the first time he saw a man in a boat who could really row and from whom he thought he could learn something was on July 4, 1870 in Buffalo.

Courtney and his friends had heard that there was to be a shell boat race on that day, so they "went to see how other people rowed," he said.

"I knew the record (for two miles) was 15:15 (15 minutes, 15 seconds) and I was rowing it two minutes faster than that. We had an accurately surveyed two-mile course—out and back—and I had made it in 13:10," he said. "I therefore went up to Buffalo to see how those other fellows were rowing. I was surprised to see how slow they went. I began to think that perhaps I could row," he concluded.

From Courtney and Cornell Rowing

Charles Courtney at age eighteen.

From the History of Cayuga County, 1879.

CHAPTER 2

CARPENTER AND OARSMAN

During the next decade, Courtney earned his living as a carpenter and gained a reputation for doing very good work. He also became an expert amateur oarsman, renowned for his ability and his devotion to the sport.

"That big Courtney boy," as he had been called around Union Springs, was soon a tall, dark-haired and handsome young man, confident that he was good at his trade and good at rowing, but still, in many respects, the countryman, unfamiliar with sophisticated society and unprepared to deal with its more aggressive factions. After learning the carpentry trade from Silas Ludlow and working with Jerry Jaquith, a carpenter, and with Emmet Anthony, an architect, Courtney went into business with his brother John F., under the name of Courtney Brothers.

Their brother James T. went to California. Another brother, William H., died in Andersonville Prison, having been captured by the Confederate forces with thirty-nine others in Captain Angel's command, west of Newbern, North Carolina, during the Civil War. Their sister Carrie was matron at "The Shelter" in Syracuse for many years. Their sister Alice married James Larmon.

An advertisement in the *Union Springs Advertiser* of January 25, 1872 listed the brothers John and Charles Courtney, as "carpenters and builders, prepared to take contracts and execute jobs on the most favorable terms. Building or repairing done by the day when desired. Stair casing a specialty. A large stock of sash, blinds, doors and mouldings constantly on hand. Shop (at) corner Chapel and Salem Streets, Union Springs." The Courtney brothers also

Photo by author

made the Thomas buckwheat huller that was very popular.

Besides making the accessories of the building trade, such as sashes, doors, blinds and hubs, Charles Courtney is credited with inventing and building a self-propelled cart for children, called the "Irish Mail." By moving the handle back and forward, a child could travel along in the cart without needing someone to pull it.

The Courtney brothers were the carpenters for the Union Springs Village Hall, approved by the village trustees in 1874 to replace the facilities that were destroyed by fire in 1873. The new brick and wood structure was built from drawings made by Charles Courtney. Then he and his brother received $1,300 for doing the carpentry. They also built several houses in the area.

Charles was an accomplished cabinetmaker. A dining table with six leaves, made of maple, was among the cherished family possessions. Other things, mentioned by his neice, Nellie Larmon Anthony, are a child's doll bed and a library table.

The Courtney brothers' shop was near their house at 6 Chapel Street where they lived with their mother. She was a short woman who could stand under Charlie's extended arm and who was fondly called "Charlie's little mother" by the many friends of the boys who were often welcomed to their home.

Industries and businesses in Union Springs and the Town of Springport at this time included several mills—saw mills, flour and grist mills, and plaster mill. There were limestone and gypsum quarries nearby, and in town, a cooper shop, creamery, foundry where stoves and farm implements were made, brick and tile works, tannery, blacksmith shop and

From Courtney and Cornell Rowing

The Courtney homestead.

several merchants handling a variety of merchandise.

Although these trades and businesses flourished, the main attractions to outsiders were the boating opportunities and the springs that had water with a strong taste of sulphur, believed to be very healthful. This was the era of steamboats and large summer resort hotels along the lakes, which attracted a clientele eager to escape the cities in the summer. Cayuga Lake, like many of the lakes in New York State and elsewhere, had a great deal of steamboat traffic because it was the best way to transport people, freight and mail from one community to another. This meant business for boat builders, many of whom lived in the towns along the lake, including Union Springs. Some of the hotels had their own, smaller steamers. There were steam-operated ferry boats, too. Some of the steamboat schedules on Cayuga Lake were arranged to connect with railroad train stops at Ithaca and elsewhere. At Union Springs, canal boats were made for use on the local canals that connected some of the ponds with the lake, providing easy transportation for products of the various mills. Commercial boating was a big enterprise.

In the late 1860s and early 1870s, interest in rowing spread rapidly throughout America. Yacht racing was already a big summer sport on the inland lakes. And horse racing continued to be popular. But rowing in single sculls, double-sculls, paired oars, and four-, six- and finally eight-oared shells very soon became a leading attraction for spectators and participants. The newspapers caught on fast, and soon gave the oarsmen top coverage. The steamboats advertised transportation to the starting and finishing lines for the races. The railroads quickly realized that rowing competitions were good ways to increase patronage. They advertised special fares to the regatta sites and special rates on observation cars that ran on railroad spurs built especially to follow the race course. Occasionally a railroad would put up prize money for a race. Gamblers took every opportunity to pursue their trade.

Although the young men in Union Springs were unfamiliar with shell and paper boats in 1868, rowing as a sport, professional and amateur, had been popular in some areas of this country for a couple of decades and had had a longer tradition in England. The first races are said to have originated in 1716 in England when Thomas Doggett, the actor, endowed annual races with prizes for the watermen on the River Thames who rowed him to work, as a way of showing his gratitude to them. Later in the 18th century, similar races between watermen in New York harbor launched racing in the United States. Races between the watermen at the harbors in this country increased and led to racing between individuals, clubs and colleges.

The early boats were called clinkers or lapstreak, after the way they were made. This was a method of planking in which the lower edge of the plank overlaps the upper edge of the one below it. Soon outriggers were invented. Then to make the boats lighter, boatmakers soon made the bodies of one skin of very thin wood, less than a fourth of an inch thick, over the framework. By 1868 paper boats, long and slender, were being made of several sheets of heavy white paper that were laminated together with glue or varnish. They were considered the fanciest of the racing boats, many of them made by the Waters Paper Boat Company of Troy.

The oars in the early boats where held on the gunwales with thole pins. The oarsmen sat on fixed seats. The thole pins were replaced by metal outriggers which hold the oarlock out from the side of the boat. The stationary seats were replaced by seats that slid on runners. Later these seats were put on small rollers.

After Courtney's victory in 1868 over the oarsmen in two shell boats, rowing "took hold" in the Springs, he said. He and his friends formed the Union Springs Boat Club. Such boat clubs for oarsmen were common in that era, organized and sustained by the communities they represented. They competed against each other and against college crews at some regattas. The Detroit Boat Club, founded in 1839, is the oldest in this country.

By the time of the Civil War, some oarsmen, single and double scullers, were able to earn a living by racing for money, the prizes being provided by businesses, individuals or communities. The competition was informal, with individuals, colleges, and clubs in the various races at regattas. The distinction between amateur and professional was not very clear until 1872 when the oarsmen who rowed "for the fun of it" took a stand against those who rowed for money, and formed the National Association of Amateur Oarsmen. This organization set the qualifications for being an amateur, which essentially were that a person must not row for money but for the pleasure of it in leisure hours and not teach it for a livelihood.

During the early 1870s Charles Courtney rowed in local races and quickly gained a reputation as a powerful oarsman. He practiced whenever he could in various boats of his own manufacture as well as on the machine he invented and used at his workshop. He and his brother John were members of the Union Springs crew that was also becoming noted for winning races. Their boathouse on the shore of Cayuga Lake near the steamboat landing was a mecca for oarsmen on the lake.

During these years Cornell University was still young, having been established in 1865 and formally opened in September of 1868. The students, who had a strong interest in the popular sport of rowing, were eager to take on some of the rowing clubs along Cayuga Lake. The day they raced against the Union Springs Rowing Club crew and its leading oarsman, Charles Courtney, is described by C. V. Young in his book, *Courtney And Cornell Rowing.* The account indicates the prowess of the young men from the rowing club "up the lake" at Union Springs in the Town of Springport. Young quotes the sports writer of *The Cornell Era* of a later day:

> Charley Courtney was the stroke of that memorable crew, and that explains what follows. The Cornell crew stroked by Dole, the trainer who had been secured to prepare a crew for the Intercollegiate Regatta, with Dutton, Goldsmith and Bean the other members. The boat used by the University crew was named *The Buffalo* and was supposed to be quite a triumph of the boat-builder's art, while the boat used by the other crew, *The Sam Weller,* was thirty or forty inches wide and loomed up like a canal-boat. She had been specially selected (by the Cornellians) for the Springport crew because it was thought that no four men could bail her out and at the same time propel her fast enough to win a race. No wonder that as that 'big four' came sweeping in ahead of our boys, we stared at them in silent wonder.
>
> The second race was for single scullers and we had only one, Jack Elseffer, but he had not lost a race, or even been hard-pressed in tryouts. His antagonist was Charley Courtney. Poor Jack rowed as if his life were at stake, and he evidently thought there was a chance for him to win, for he was never more than a few feet behind the other boat. In the following years, when Charley swept all the amateur scullers before him, we understood better why it was that Jack could not overcome that exasperating lead.

There is no record of the other three men on that victorious Union Springs crew, but a few years later the crew was composed of: Collins, bow; Winegar, 2; J. F. Courtney, 3; C. Courtney, stroke. These men won numerous races on Cayuga and Seneca lakes.

An interesting comment on the earnest endeavors of the young amateur oarsmen from Union Springs was reported by William F. Courtney, John F. Courtney's son, when he wrote to Gould P. Colman, Cornell University archivist, in 1972. William F. Courtney was reminiscing about his uncle, Charles Courtney and wrote:

> Going back to the early days of rowing before there was the roller sliding seat, my father [John F.] told me about the crew from Union Springs of which he was a member along with my uncle. [They] polished up some cherry boards which they coated with butter at the start of the race. They worked because Union Springs won.

By the spring of 1873, Charles Courtney was becoming well-known in the lake district as a powerful oarsman. Although he was busy at the carpentry trade, earning a dollar a day, he found time to practice rowing, either alone or with the Union Springs crew, which he coached.

Even though he had beaten the Cornell student in 1872, Courtney didn't consider that event of much significance. Instead, he considered the next race of any note after the 1868 race at Aurora, to be the three-mile race at Syracuse on June 25, 1873, when he beat two entries from New York by a quarter of a mile. The prize was a gold watch, which he wore for twenty-two years.

"In that race I had a lapstreak boat, twenty-three feet long and nineteen inches wide. I got her at Geneva," he said.

Saratoga was probably the most fashionable summer resort in the east at this time. Horse racing, the healthful waters from the springs, the social life and the gambling attracted large crowds of city-dwellers. And now that rowing was becoming a popular sport, the small, eight-mile long lake was being promoted as an ideal site for sculling contests.

A young man from Union Springs, who was working at the Grand Union Hotel at Saratoga, mentioned Charlie Courtney to the right people at Saratoga. Soon Courtney was invited to compete in a race in September. Accepting the invitation was a momentous decision for Courtney; he would need regular a racing shell, which cost $126.

"I was still learning my trade at a dollar a day and paying for my board, and it wasn't an easy matter to raise the money," he said. "The boys chipped in, of course. The folks around town helped me some, and Dr. (Benjamin) Fordyce generously took our note for a loan of forty dollars to make up the balance. It was the first regular racing shell I ever owned. It was twelve inches wide, thirty feet long and weighed thirty pounds," he said.

Even though Courtney had raced against men from the cities and had had some contact with wealthy sportsmen who were summer residents along Cayuga Lake, he was naive about the customs of sophisticated society. His own account of his first experience at Saratoga shows the bewilderment that faced the young countryman from Union Springs. He said:

> I left for Saratoga with fifteen dollars in my pocket and that, I reckoned, ought to pay my board for at least three weeks. I got there and went right to the [Grand Union] hotel and saw my young friend. Then I went to the desk and asked the clerk about the price of board, and when he told me three dollars and a half a day, I nearly dropped. I went into the dining room and was about half scared to death. I had never been far away from home for any length of time, and I felt so awkward and green that I imagined every one was looking at me; I simply couldn't eat, hungry as I was. If I reached for a fork, I stuck my fingers into the butter, the soup was so hot I burned my tongue, and reaching for a glass of water, I knocked over the celery dish, and things were a mess. The waiter glared at me. I thought the best thing for me to do was to bolt; so out I rushed, feeling that I had made myself a laughing stock. I walked along the lake, and about the time I cooled down, I came to Moon's Hotel. That looked good to me, and in I went.
>
> There I met an old friend, John Morrissey, who immediately took me under his wing. He introduced me to Mr. [Charles] Moon, and we sat down at the family table. While Morrissey told us about his history and his early training, I ate. I shall never forget that dinner—biscuits, brook trout, black bass, partridge—everything that was good, and I was so interested in the conversation that I never noticed until afterwards that the others had long finished and were just watching me eat.
>
> Well, in a few days I got a little more used to things, and was soon busy practicing for the race. When I wasn't rowing, I was out back of the boathouse lying in the grass, as I didn't like to be stared at as one fresh from the country. It had been noised around how green I was. But Mr. Morrissey ever after looked out for me. He never failed to come each day, or to send someone to see how I was getting along.
>
> But I was far from comfortable with only fifteen dollars in my pocket and board $3.50 a day. I plucked up courage one day and told Mr. Moon how much money I had and that I thought I would have to go home. You see, we were there some eight days before the race, training every day. Mr. Moon looked at me and said: "Lord bless you, young man, I'll see that you get back to Union Springs, and see that you don't have to walk, either." This relieved

me, so that I was able to sleep nights.

Mr. Morrissey didn't have any bets on the race, but Mr. Moon did. There were thirteen starters—twelve besides myself. An unlucky number? Lucky enough for me. There was quite a number who had come down from Union Springs. The Albany people were backing a fellow named Wilson. They had a pretty high opinion of him, but there didn't anybody at the outset seem to think enough to bet any money on me, though I told the folks from home I could win; I knew I could.

Every day crowds gathered on the docks around the lake and filled pleasure boats to watch the contestants practice. The spectators would talk with the oarsmen and trainers, notice what the athletes ate and how well they "pulled an oar." Then there would be long discussions on which oarsman was the best bet. Some of these spectators put money on Courtney, as he was surprised to learn after the race. He said:

It was a beautiful day on which the race was rowed, and it must have been a great sight to see those thirteen men in line and thirteen pairs of oars flash in the sunlight.

When I think back over it all, I have to smile at some of the funny things that occurred. I was pretty nervous at the start, and I started out to row as if it were a hundred-yard sprint. My boat went ahead so fast that spectators began to yell, "Whoa, whoa!" and I could hear them laugh, but I thought they were making fun of me and I rowed all the harder. When I got down to Ramsdall's Point I was so far ahead that a young man, who had a lady in a boat with him, asked me if I wouldn't stop and take a drink of lemonade. "You have time enough," he said, but of course I rowed all the harder, Courtney recalled.

Everybody at home had told me I would be beaten, and I was wondering every stroke if someone would catch me. But no one did, and I won by over a quarter of a mile. The time was 14:15, which was one minute faster than Josh Ward's [professional] record. They all thought it was a wonderful performance, but I had a minute up my sleeve even then, if the water had been smooth, he said.

The regatta was considered a complete success by others, too. There was no pool selling, a great deviation from the usual custom at regattas. The *Ithaca Journal* gave more prominence to the lack of betting pools than to the winners of the races. It seems the Young Men's Christian Association and the Rowing

Association were trying to "clean up" the gambling that frequently prevailed, bringing unsavory gamblers to the regatta sites. In language characteristic of the era, the newspaper reported:

> SARATOGA, N.Y.—Sept. 11—The regatta was a complete success. The attendance was very large and the facilities for observing the races were universally approved. The weather was favorable and the water in capital condition.
>
> There was no pool selling allowed here, the Young Men's Christian Association having prevented it in town and the Rowing Association having effectually stopped it at the lake. No persons expressed more sincere satisfaction with this arrangement than the various (rowing) clubs themselves. They say they do not wish to be placed on a level with horses. Several of them informed Mr. Conkling, the president of the Rowing Association, that if pool selling was allowed they would not dip an oar.

Pool selling may not have been allowed, but some people made money by betting on Courtney and shared their profits with the husky, young oarsman from the country. He said:

> After the race I went up to pay my board, and asked what the bill was. "Well, young man," said Mr. Moon, "come with me into the sitting-room and we'll settle up." We went in and he sat down at a table and pulled out a roll of bills and counted them out. "There!" he said, I won three hundred dollars on this race—you take half of it." He insisted upon my taking the money, and he didn't charge me a cent for board besides, and then he hitched up his horses and took me and my boat back to Saratoga.
>
> Then [before Courtney left the hotel] James H. Brister of Union Springs came to my room and said he had placed a little on the race and as I had done all the work I ought to have a share in the result. He had won six hundred dollars and gave me half of it. I felt like a Rothschild. I never had too much money before. I left Saratoga with $450 in my pocket, besides the fifteen dollars I had brought. I tell you, I never let go of that money until I got home.
>
> Mother was glad I won, and the money helped, but she was afraid it might lead me on to other races. She had opposed my racing from the beginning; all of the family, except my brother John, were opposed to it, too.

The regatta at Saratoga showed Courtney that he could row as well as the best oarsmen, and it opened his eyes to a world that was much more sophisticated than the village of Union Springs. It also brought him to the attention of sporting fans. Soon he was invited to regattas throughout the eastern United States.

Despite the opposition of his family, Courtney continued to row. He entered eighty-eight races as an amateur and never lost a race.

Cornell Archives

Charles Courtney on Frontenac Beach,
Union Springs in the late 1870s.

CHAPTER 3

CHAMPION OARSMAN

After the Saratoga Regatta of 1873, the word spread rapidly that Charles Courtney, the countryman from Union Springs, could really row. At home he continued to do carpentry work and to train the local young men in the Union Springs Boat Club, which had a boathouse on the lake shore where the young men gathered to row after work and on weekends.

The telegraph wires supplied the local newspapers in Ithaca and Auburn with reports of races of professional and amateur oarsmen. Among the leading professionals were the Ward brothers and the Biglin brothers, the latter immortalized by the famous American painter, Thomas Eakins, who painted them in racing form about 1873. The rowing fever was spreading. The amateurs adopted the customs of the professionals, including costumes to distinguish them from other oarsmen; clubs had their own colors. And lakeside communitiies soon recognized the economic advantages of having a regatta nearby. Regattas brought visitors by train and by boat who stayed in local hotels, hired conveyances from local livery stables, and generally spent money in the regatta town. One of these communities was Watkins Glen, at the southern end of Seneca Lake, the lake west of Cayuga in central New York.

The Watkins and Seneca Lake Regatta Association staged its first regatta on September 9, 10 and 11, 1874. It attracted racing yachts, single scullers, boat clubs with four-oared crews and college crews. The day before the races, the *Ithaca Journal* predicted great success for the regatta. "Watkins was alive with excitement in reference to the coming races—the hotels were densely thronged. . . . Many people from distant parts of the state arrived in town. . . . Everything betokens a great turnout and the complete success of the first annual regatta on Senaca." And on the first day, the account said, "The number of people in attendance on the first day, in a region of the state where a regatta of any importance or significance was never heard of before, may be regarded as very satisfactory." An estimated 10,000 people viewed the races, the *Ithaca Journal* noted in its final round up story of the regatta, which like most of its reports of the regatta, was condensed from accounts in the *Elmira Advertiser.*

A report of the weather introduced each newspaper account of the regatta. The first day's report, was: "The day dawned with magnificent weather and a cloudless sky and continued until after the races were concluded. . . . The wind was light and the lake in excellent condition for shells and sculls. . . . The water was smooth and clear, and it seemed as if Neptune himself was laboring to make this delightful affair successful."

By 1874, the Union Springs Rowing Club had a colorful costume, which, like those of others, consisted of close-fitting pants that reached the knees, a sleeveless shirt and often a snug cap or a kerchief tied around the head. They had a shell boat and were referred to as the "Courtney crew of Union Springs."

The appearance of the four-oared crews of the boat clubs at the starting line was a brilliant sight. "The Courtney crew were the first to make their appearance, shooting out from the float like an arrow from a bow. They claim they never sat in a boat as a crew before and that they had no hope of winning the race, and as it happened, they were not disappointed. Their colors were blue and white," the reporter wrote.

The next crew to appear for the lineup was the Seneca Falls crew, "a fine, muscular set of fellows who swung well together but who had an ancient boat. They were followed by the Stars of Rochester, who came rushing out from the float clad in magenta suits, altogether making such a pretty show that the crowds which thronged the judges' boat, *Estelle,* and

Cornell Archives

This crew won at Watkins, in 1875, Courtney wrote on this picture. The boat was built by E. L. Phillips. In the boat are: bow, Collins; No. 2, Winegar; No. 3, J. F. Courtney; stroke, C. Courtney, stroke.

the surrounding steamers were quite taken with them. They, however, had a rival in the Rochester Riversides, who were neatly clad in dark blue, and of course created a sensation, as they took their place in line," the newspaper account related. No description was given of the fifth entry, the Buffalo Boat Club's crew, which was the winner with the Courtney boat from Union Springs a close second.

One of the big attractions of this first Watkins Regatta, was the appearance of Charles Courtney, called "the great single sculler" whom the newspaper reporter expected to "take time by the forelock" and make the best time on record.

Courtney's skill as an oarsman brought him enemies as well as acclaim. One of these adversaries, James Riley, appeared at the Watkins Regatta and continued to antagonize him through his amateur and professional rowing career.

When the four contestants in the amateur senior scull race lined up, Riley was there also but on the outside of the buoys. He was not permitted to compete because he was not an amateur and was disqualified. He said he wanted to row alongside the contestants to show boatmen, as he had often boasted, along with his backers, that "he could beat the champion Courtney so bad he would never show himself again."

Courtney's power, skill and method of rowing impressed the spectators. Right after the start it immediately became clear that he would not have the slightest difficulty in winning. "He quickly took the front, pulling a peculiar stroke of his own, unlike any other which we have ever seen," the reporter wrote. "His reach is long, about six feet nine inches, and the manner in which he catches the water shows a master hand, the oar blade going in as keenly as a knife without the slightest sign of a splash. The pull through the water is slow, steady and herculean, ending as clean as it began, and the recovery is as measured as the pull."

Courtney kept far in advance of the others, without any apparent effort, rounding the stake 17 seconds before Riley and considerably ahead of the other contestants, who were Courtney's brother John, Robert H. Robinson of Union Springs, and W. E. McCrady. There was scarcely any excitement on the home stretch, but Riley taunted Courtney and egged him on. "Courtney only dipped deeper and pulled stronger and the light shell bounded like a dart from him, leaving Riley discomfited and disheartened twenty-five or thirty lengths behind . . . Courtney won (the two-mile race) in 14 minutes 10 seconds. . . . This, the winning time, was only 17 seconds short of the fastest on record and was made without a spurt on Courtney's part. "Had he pulled his best and laid himself in it, he would not only have beaten it by a good deal but would have left his contestants so far behind that they would hardly dare tackle him again. As it was, it was a beautiful race, and alone well worth the journey to Watkins," the reporter wrote.

Other big attractions at the regatta were the races of the

six-oared boats with coxswains that were used by some of the boat clubs and by the Cornell University crews. There were also yacht races.

* * *

During the next three years Courtney continued to row and win races as an amateur, either alone or with some of his friends, often Robinson or Frank Yates, from Union Springs.

After getting the silver cup at Aurora in 1868, Courtney accumulated a variety of prizes. At Watkins in 1874 he received silver dinner set of knives, forks and spoons. For the New York State championships in 1874 and 1875 he received a silver cup and a badge. Among his other prizes were a breech loading gun, a cake basket, a fruit dish, a soup tureen, several badges, banners and cups. Some of these awards were for double scull races he rowed with Robinson.

Besides being a busy year for the Union Springs oarsmen, 1875 brought memorable events into Courtney's life. On January 28, he married Della S. Halsey of Ithaca, New York. In March, John and Charles moved their carpentry business to their new, large building, called the Central New York Planing and Hub Works. They built this on land that they had purchased from W. H. Chase near their home and closer to the lake. Here they hired fifteen to twenty men. A few years later they erected a 50– by 80–foot addition where they produced between 5,000 and 6,000 hubs and spokes a year.

In this building Charles practiced rowing on the machine he developed. Here, also, he worked on the boats he used, learning to make adjustments to suit his own rowing needs. He was very particular about details—the finish on the boat, the height of the riggers, the seat, the oars. He had found that close attention to details made the difference in a race. The experience he gained by adjusting his own boat, made him especially alert to the needs of all the Cornell oarsmen who rowed under him in later years.

Another champion practiced in the Courtneys' mill. He was William Hoagland, a close friend of Charlie, who took up heel and toe walking at Charlie's suggestion and became the national champion.

In this era, rowing became recognized as good exercise for both young men and young women. Many women's seminaries provided boats for their students to use. Garbed in bloomers, middie blouses and sailor hats, the women learned to handle the oars, and thus improve their posture, the goal of some of the educators of young ladies. Courtney was the coach of the women's crews at the schools in his village, the Quakers' Oakwood Seminary and Howland College.

It is easy to imagine the great activity at the lake shore near Union Springs in those days. Boats of all kinds were tied to the docks or plying the waters. In the daytime, women's crews were practicing, and in the evening the young men rowed. Families and friends sat along the banks or on the docks to watch the practice sessions of Courtney and the Union Springs Club. Courtney usually practiced in the protected waters of the bay near the planing mill and Frontenac Beach and in view of Frontenac Island, the only natural island in all of the Finger Lakes of New York State.

Courtney won again at the Saratoga Regatta in 1875. In a preview article, it was reported that two men have "squirted" and will not pull in the regatta because they fear Courtney in the single and Courtney and Robinson in the double. Their fears were well-founded. Courtney led the twelve entrants in the singles race right from the start. At the first half mile Courtney led, Yates second and Bainbridge third. At the turn, one mile, Courtney still led with Yates second and Riley third. On the return, at the half-mile stake, Courtney still was in front. Riley apparently qualified satisfactorily as an amateur so he could be in this race. He came in right behind Courtney who won in 13 minutes 58½ seconds.

On the next day, Courtney and Robinson won the double scull race, bringing more acclaim and attention to the oarsmen from Union Springs.

Scarcely a week later at Troy, New York, Courtney won the National Challenge Cup in single scull racing, and he and Robinson won a similar award in the doubles.

The Springs, as the village was often called, was becoming noted for its accomplished oarsmen. In fact, after victories of Cayuga Lake crews and Courtney in 1875, as well as the Cornell University crews, the *Ithaca Journal* on August 24 ran a short article suggesting that the lake's water had some miraculous power and that the water should be bottled and used as a tonic by oarsmen:

> THERE'S MILLIONS IN IT
>
> In view of Courtney's and the other victories of Cayuga Lake oarsmen, we understand that a scheme long contemplated is about to be put in execution. A large bath house is to be erected on the shores of Cayuga Lake and oarsmen from other sections are to be invited to come and bathe in the magic waters—the real fountain of youthful strength which Ponce De Leon sought in vain. It is also intended to bottle the water and derive a large revenue from its sale to the rowing clubs throughout the country who will use it as a tonic.

In May of 1875, a six-oared boat from Union Springs competed in the Cornell University Spring Day regatta and lost by 13 seconds to the University crew. But this was Cayuga oarsmen against Cayuga oarsmen, and so not considered a blot on the effectiveness of the lake's waters. In later years Courtney said, laughingly but with serious intent, that this victory by Cornell convinced him that the University's young men had some potential as oarsmen.

In early September the people of Union Springs gave a tremendous celebration for its heroes. The Ithaca reporter said, "The people were out in hearty good will. Independence Hall was thronged, and I want to say an especial good word for the collation. It was so unpretending, and so excellent, and so prettily waited upon. The victors behaved like modest, sensible gentlemen. . . . It was a proud hour for Union Springs. Her place on the map of the state is a very distinct one now. . . . Well, Cayuga Lake gives its bright record to the whole country. It wears the laurels from north to south, and Cornell and Courtney and Robinson are national words."

A few days later the local oarsmen were in Watkins for the second annual regatta on Seneca Lake. The crowds and participants were more numerous than the year before. This

Cornell Archives

Courtney's first prize trophies, won between 1868 and 1875.

THE CHAMPION'S RECORD.

FIRST PRIZES.

1. Silver Cup, at Aurora..................1868
2. French Clock, at Union Springs...... ..1869
3. Challenge Cup and Presentation Badge, at Saratoga........................1873–5
4. Gold Watch, at Syracuse...............1873
5. N. Y. State Championship Presentation Cup, at Saratoga...................1874
6. Coffee Urn, at Skaneateles.............1874
7. Silver Dinner Set (Knives, Forks and Spoons) at Watkins................ 1874
8. N. Y. State Championship Presentation Cup, at Saratoga 1875
9. N. Y. State Championship Diamond Badge, at Saratoga.......................1874–5
10. George Wilkes National Challenge Cup, at Troy...........................1875
11. Fruit Dish, at Binghamton........... 1875
12. U. S. Championship Banner, at Troy .. .1875
13. Breech Loading Parker Gun, at Aurora..1875
14. National Challenge Cup for Double Sculls, at Troy..............................1875
15. Water Set, Double, with Robinson, at Binghamton 1875
16. Cake Basket, Double, with Robinson, at Ensenore 1875
17. Soup Toureen, Double, with Robinson, at Ensenore...........................1875
18. Gold Badge, Double, with Robinson, at Saratoga..........................1875

U. S. Championship Banner, Double, with Robinson, at Troy..................1875 was said to be the first aquatic meeting where noted amateurs and professionals were so equally represented. "The streets and resorts are alive with ladies who lionize many of the oarsmen, especially Courtney and the Cornellians," the *Ithaca Journal* reporter wrote.

The evenings were full of gaiety. A large temporary dance hall had been built, and within its thin walls the sound of brass and tinkling cymbal led the dance for the sum of ten cents. The best music, however, was furnished by an Italian band at the Lake View Hotel, where brilliantly lighted parlors and verandahs and merry dancers made up a romantic scene.

"One thing is perhaps deserving of mention, and that is the common prevalence of Bibles and tracts here in some of the hotels, the Glen Mountain, for one," the reporter wrote.

Courtney announced early in the regatta session that he would not row in the amateur single sculling race, but would save himself for the four-oared race and would row alongside the professional single scullers.

The Unions Springs four-oared crew won the race in a boat that was built at the Springs with a crew that consisted of: Collins, bow; Winegar, 2; John Courtney, 3; Charles Courtney, stroke.

Courtney measured his ability as single sculler when he rowed alone alongside the professionals, among them Ellis Ward, and one of the Biglin brothers.Afterward he must have thought he could match the skills of some of the best oarsmen, because the next year he agreed to compete—as an amateur—in the Centennial International Regatta in Philadelphia.

CHAPTER 4

INTERNATIONAL CHAMPION

The news of plans for the International Regatta at the Centennial Exhibition in Philadelphia in 1876 must have aroused a great deal of interest in Union Springs. Three men, that we know of, from the village competed in the rowing events. They were Charles Courtney, R. H. Robinson and F. E. Yates. The fact that others from the Springs besides Courtney competed indicates that the young men of that village were taking rowing seriously, were practicing hard and were willing to give up time from their occupations to go to Philadelphia, probably several days ahead of the scheduled events so they could practice on the unfamiliar waters, as was customary for competitors.

The regatta was held under the auspices of the United States Centennial Commission but was under the local management of the Schuykill Navy, an organization of nine boating clubs located on the Schuykill River near Philadelphia. The leading boat clubs of the United States, Britain, the English universities and the City of London competed. The elaborate prizes for amateurs, presented by the Centennial Commission, included delicately crafted vases, punch bowls, tureens and medals in gold, silver and bronze, most of them having designs with a national or nautical theme. A special diamond badge was prepared for the winner of single-shell race. Cash prizes were given to the professional winners.

The race course was considered one of the best in the world because the river was broad, deep and still, and without obstacles to interrupt the participants.

The International Regatta was in progress from August 22 to September 6. The first three days were devoted to the

Cornell Archives

Frank Yates, left, and Charles Courtney in 1876. They often raced together in double sculls.

National Association of Amateur Oarsmen's fourth annual regatta, staged over the same course as the international event.

The international races had four categories: first, an international race for all regularly organized boat clubs in the world for four-oared boats, for pairs, for double sculls and for single sculls; second, an international college race for four-oared shells, open only to undergraduates; third, an international graduates race open only to graduates of colleges and universities; and fourth, professional races, open to all professional crews throughout the world for four-oared, pair-oared and single scull shells.

All races were rowed in heats, which had become a common practice by 1876 because there were so many entries in the regattas. The amateur races were one and a half miles straightaway, and the professional were three miles with a turn at the one and a half mile mark.

These probably were some of the instructions and conditions that the young men in Union Springs read when they sent for information about the regatta. There were entrance fees, which were refunded to all the entrants starting in the races, but were considered necessary as guarantees of good faith and to help the committee, largely from the Schuykill Navy, in making arrangements for housing the participants. Also, oarsmen from the Springs had to go by train to Philadelphia and take their boats and be away from their jobs for about ten days. Altogether the trip to the Centennial races probably was an expensive project.

The biggest crowd ever to attend an American regatta up to that time went to Philadelphia. It was estimated that a million people filled grandstands at the finish line, thronged the shore line and sat in pleasure boats and on docks along the course.

The members of the Schuykill Navy assumed many of the details for the regatta and contributed liberally to the expenses of the fete, which, unlike the Exhibition itself, brought no financial return to the sponsors. The Philadelphians furnished quarters in their own boathouses for the boats of the visiting competitors and erected temporary boathouses in the park, which furnished ample accomodations to all who came to take part in the races.

We assume that the young men from Union Springs wore the colors of their club, blue and white. And so would have been part of the "brilliant scene," as one reporter described the regatta. Winners were greeted with "deafening cheers" when they came in. The regatta was called a brilliant success.

The young men from Union Springs made a fine showing, taking home several trophies, the most prestigious being the bejeweled badge that Courtney won as the International Amateur Single Sculls champion. But that victory was one of the final events of the regatta.

During the first days, the races in the fourth annual National Association of Amateur Oarsmen's competition were held over the race course. Yates from the Springs won the single sculls national prize, and Robinson and Courtney won the double sculls national award.

The International Regatta began on August 28, with several trial heats in each category. In the first round of trial heats, Robinson placed second in the third heat for single sculls. The next day Courtney was matched against three other men, two of whom withdrew, leaving Courtney and P. C. Ackerman of the Atalanta Club in New York to row the course. Then Ackerman got sick and did not go over the course, according to the *Ithaca Journal* reporter who was at the scene. Courtney rowed the course in 11 minutes 29¾ seconds, a slow time for him. In the fifth heat, a Union Springs oarsman, Yates, beat his three opponents, with the time of 12 minutes 5½ seconds.

The first event announced for the fourth day was the first heat in the second round trial heats for single sculls. Courtney was to row against Yates, S. J. Gormley and F. Pleasanton of the Quaker City Boat Club of Philadelphia. All three opponents withdrew, leaving Courtney to row the course alone. He pulled leisurely over the course in 10 minutes 32½ seconds. The Ithaca newsman wrote:

> It seemed a great pity that the skill and muscle of our Cayuga Lake hero could not be exhibited during this international aquatic contest by meeting some sculler who would oblige him to work to gain victory. As it has been only inferior oarsmen who have entered the lists against him, Charlie has had regular walk-overs. With his characteristic generosity, he has rowed simply fast enough to win his heats and not disgrace his competitors by beating them badly. This fact, in addition to his genial and affable manners towards all with whom he has come in contact, has made him a general favorite here, and he will ever be welcome on the banks of the Schuykill.

That same day, Courtney secured the international championship by beating James McCartney of the Friendship Club of Friendship, New York. Courtney's time was 10 minutes 48½ seconds, while McCartney did the course in 11 minutes 12½ seconds. "Without really an effort, our Cayuga Lake sculler won the first prize in the grand international regatta, and the amateur championship of the world," noted the reporter.

Disappointment that the single sculling contests had not been more lively showed up in the newspaper columns. "He (Courtney) came here expecting to measure blades with the

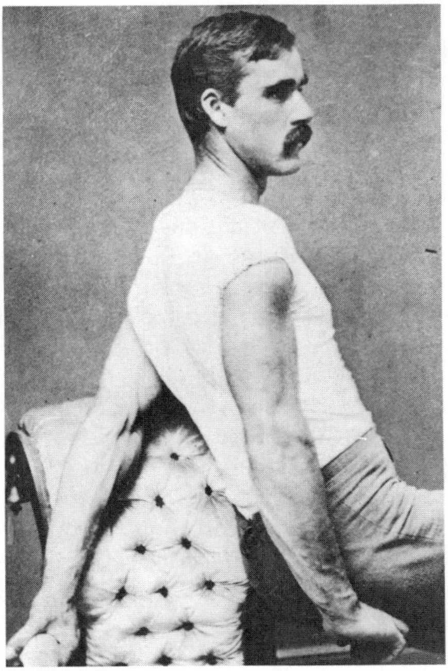

Charles Courtney, age 26, in 1875.

Englishmen who crossed the ocean to row the double and single scull races in the regatta, but found Charlie too rapid for them, perhaps, and they ingloriously withdrew from the contests. But Courtney, knowing the people here were very much disappointed at this, sent them a challenge," the news account said.

Challenges were a common method of setting up races, either for a championship or for a prize. Sometimes the challenges were offered to provide races that would be pleasing to the spectators and draw crowds for whatever purposes the promoters had in mind. Challenges were especially common in professional competition, which Courtney would find out later had many pitfalls.

Courtney and Yates sent a written statement to the London Boat Club crew that said the Americans challenged the Britishers to a single scull race and a double scull race. The complete text that appeared in the *Ithaca Journal* follows:

It is addressed to Messrs. Frank B. Gulston and R. H. Labat, Park View Hotel, Philadelphia, Pa. and is dated September 1, 1876.

> Gentlemen:
>
> We hereby challenge you both to row us in the following races on the terms herein named:
>
> First—A single scull, straightaway one mile and a half contest, over the international course on the Schuykill River, at any time during your present stay in this country; either one of us to row either one of you; your two names to be put in one hat, our two in another, representatives to draw, and the man on your side whose names is drawn first to row him on the other side whose name is drawn first, and the two others to row each other immediately after the first two drawn have rowed their race.
>
> Second—A double scull race, same course and distance, on any day during your stay, except that immediately preceding or following that of said single scull contest; you two to row us two. In each contest you have the choice of position. Should you desire to have prizes given in these races we stand ready to contribute one half of their value.
>
> This is handed you on the day of its dates, and we should be pleased to have you reply during the present week.
>
> Charles E. Courtney
> F. E. Yates

"The above challenge," the reporter said,

> on being handed Captain Gulston, was flatly and emphatically declined on the grounds that the crew would be obliged to leave for England shortly. Your correspondent has since ascertained that they do not intend sailing before the middle of the month. What this means I leave the intelligent readers of the *Journal* to imagine for themselves.

The next day, the fifth day of heats in the amateur portion of the regatta, Courtney and Yates won the second heat in the double sculls contest and went on to win the final heat in double sculls with the time of 9 minutes 52½ seconds.

With the amateur races finished, the professionals began their races. One of the contestants and a winner would, within two years, be the toughest opponent Courtney would ever meet. His name was Edward Hanlan, a young, dark-haired Canadian, six years younger than Courtney, and just as popular in Canada as Courtney was in the United States. Hanlan won the professional single scull three-mile race in 21 minutes 9 seconds. He easily took the lead in every heat he entered, and was quickly called one of the best single scullers of all time.

Like Courtney, Hanlan had grown up near the water. His home was on the island in Toronto Bay where his father ran a hotel. He, too, had raced in little boats as a child, in fishermen's skiffs later, and in 1873, like Courtney, had obtained his first shell boat. Hanlan rowed in races, generally in Canada, beating his challengers and earning local awards, including the Ontario championship in 1876. That same year he had attracted sufficient attention that a group of men formed the Hanlan Club to guide his career. The Hanlan Club entered him in the Centennial Regatta, and with the rest of the world, was astounded at his amazing speed.

The American public was eager to hear more about the young Canadian, and the Hanlan Club was happy to oblige with plenty of publicity. Various schemes were staged to arouse interest in the club's oarsman and whoever was his opponent. For example, a railroad whistle-stop tour attracted large crowds to see the oarsmen and netted cash for them. Special fares were promoted, and the newspapers invariably called Hanlan's races "The Great Race." He was given a hero's welcome whenever he returned to Toronto from a race, which he always seemed to win. Within the next decade he rowed in America many times and several times in England and then in Australia. He was Canada's first international sports hero.

In the late fall of 1876 Courtney announced that he would henceforth row as a professional. It was inevitable that he and Hanlan would race each other, but the beginning of their encounters would be nearly two years in the future.

The 1877 rowing season, Courtney's first as a professional oarsman, was a rough initiation for him into the world of professional sports.

CHAPTER 5

COURTNEY POISONED

Many years later, after Courtney had finished his professional rowing career and was a coach at Cornell, he was asked, "Why did you abandon the amateur field and start in as a professional in 1877?"

> Because I was a fool, he replied. I had no more business in the professional line than I had of being a preacher. I was simply led into it—urged on by my friends. I had reached a point in my career where nature was asserting her rights. I had trained for eighty-eight races (and won them all) and that ought to have satisfied any man's ambition. I was satisfied, too, but it must be remembered that I was young, and my eye-teeth were not as long as they are now.
>
> I had rowed for nine years. I was still a young man—about twenty-eight—but I was no longer capable of always doing my best work. I had a sunstroke, and never was the man I was before that. There were days when I could row a race that would bother any man, but there were other days when I could not do myself justice. Dr. Van Cleve told me, at Watkins, that I had trained to a point where I had to stop or I would kill myself. I thought not. I had gotten into it and thought I could wriggle out of it, but the more I wriggled the deeper I got in.

The year 1877 was in the era of large resort hotels, located on the shores of inland lakes. Summer visitors came from the large cities by train to the stations on the lake. Then they often had to travel by steamboat to the hotel's dock where the big trunks and suitcases were unloaded and carried up to the hotel. The high-ceilinged, ornate hotels had wide verandahs where visitors could sit and watch the activity on the lake.

The long, voluminous skirts and wide hats worn by the female visitors did not deter them from going to the dock and boarding pleasure boats, or from taking a horse and buggy to ride around the countryside. Watching the sculling races was a popular pastime for the thousands of summer visitors.

Wherever there was a regatta with its many spectators, there were peddlers of food and drink. There were hucksters of souvenirs, such as handkerchiefs and pennants representing the colors and insignia of the competing oarsmen, as well as their pictures on banners. And most notorious in the crowds were the gamblers. They had learned their trade at such events as horse races, boxing matches, steamboat and yacht races, and they easily adapted their skills to the new craze—rowing.

A gambler was easy to identify. He usually wore a black, knee-length frock coat and black hat, sometimes it was a derby. His shirt probably had a ruffle down the front and on the cuffs. He was sure to be sporting a diamond or two, either on his rings, or lapel or stickpin. A gold watch with a long gold chain was his trademark. Some of the gamblers ran betting pools and others set up their tents with games of chance. Pickpockets and thieves also were at the regattas in force.

This was the atmosphere at one of the races early in Courtney's professional career. In the middle of July 1877 he was scheduled to race James Riley, the professional oarsman, who had been disqualified as an amateur at the 1876 Centennial Regatta. The race, on Greenwood Lake in New Jersey, attracted large crowds from the metropolitan areas. It promised to be an exciting race in a beautiful setting, but the newspaper accounts the day afterward were headlined "Courtney Poisoned."

The reporter from the *Auburn Daily Advertiser* described the pastoral setting in glowing terms:

> The view from the summit of the mountain (Greenwood) is truly a gorgeous spectacle, and as we reined in our horse . . . we had the whole valley of Warwick before us, a little to the right Mount Adam and Mount Eve, and still beyond in misty outline, the broken line of the Catskills.
>
> Greenwood Lake, formerly called Long Pond, is nine miles long, three and a half miles being in Passaic County, New Jersey and five and a half miles in Orange County, New York. Its greatest width is one mile. The foot of the lake has been dammed up and is

> used as a feeder by the Morris and Essex Canal. Its shores are skirted with timber its entire length. . . . Brown's Hotel is the only one near the foot of the Lake. The Montclair and Greenwood Railway terminus is a few miles up the lake on the opposite side while the summer resort proper and large hotels are at the extreme head of the lake, reached from the railroad by steamer. It was at the railway terminus that Courtney and Riley were to meet (for the race).
>
> The accomodations at this point are of the most meager description, only one hotel and that a common, hastily constructed hemlock shanty, presided over by Mr. Samson George.

The *Ithaca Journal* reporter said extra trains brought crowds of people who filled the wharf and the lone covered passage leading up the hill, then they swarmed over the green slopes. New York City had sent a large delegation of its "toughest" citizens. Thieves, swindlers, gamblers and ruffians of every sort were there. All sorts of devices for entrapping the unwary visitor were in full blast. There were at least a dozen wheels-of-fortune, several three-card monte tables and a number of wooden men with movable heads, at which, on payment of a fee, the greenhorn might throw baseballs with a promise of a bad cigar in the event of success. There were two pool-selling booths. Lager beer, lemonade, sandwiches, peanuts and gingersnaps were on sale in roughly improvised stands and out of baskets everywhere.

Respectable people were instinctively moved to undo their watch chains and hide away their watches in some secret recess, or to button their coats tightly. . . . Several detectives moved among the throng. . . . "They forced the return of a watch that an old fool had staked on his ability to tell which was the queen card," the newsman continued.

Most of the crowd of nearly 4,000 stayed on the hill overlooking the race course. Many more were in boats, on the docks and along the shore, ready for the race to begin late in the afternoon. The steamer *Montclair* brought people from the resort hotels Windemere, Brandon and Lakeside at the northern end of the lake, who would watch the race from the steamer. While the spectators were gathering for the race in this beautiful setting, few of them were aware of what had happened to one of the contestants.

Courtney had had his headquarters at the Windermere, but, due to the great distance from the race course at the other end of the lake, he had not been able to row over it. Therefore, on Friday, the day before the race, he had moved to Brown's Hotel, run by Mr. George and referred to as a "shanty hotel," at the lower end of the lake and near the course, which he rowed over in a practice run Saturday morning, the day of the race.

About five o'clock the word spread through the crowds on shore that Courtney had been taken ill suddenly and could not row. Excited groups of people gathered outside Brown's Hotel, wanting to know the whole story and the prospects for having the race.

"Up to noon today Courtney was in magnificent condition. He said he never felt so well before a race in his life. Three or four of his intimate friends and backers were at the little hotel with him, keeping a close guard over his interests," the Ithaca reporter wrote.

"They all sat down to dinner together at 12:20 o'clock, and Courtney ate a hearty meal, the principal dish being mutton. After dinner he called the waiter girl and said that he would like a glass of ice tea. All his friends agree that the hotel proprietor, Mr. Geoge, stopped the girl, saying that she did not know how to make it, and that he would make it himself. He did so, and handed the mixture to Courtney, who drank only part of it, saying, 'That's the worst tea I ever drank.' A moment afterward he said, 'I feel very bad,' and rising from his chair, vomited his entire dinner, " the reporter's account continued.

Courtney immediately fell into a state of collapse and had to be assisted upstairs and put to bed. A fierce pain attacked him in the pit of the stomach and gradually a burning sensation mounted to his throat, remaining there. His hands and feet became cold and clammy, tears ran from his bloodshot eyes, and a cold perspiration broke out on his forehead. Finally he fell into a complete stupor, from which it was impossible to rouse him, even with vigorous shaking. This description was in the special dispatch to the *New York Times.*

Messengers had been sent for physicians and medicine, but it was two hours before Dr. Olcott, who lived across the lake, arrived. One of the afternoon trains brought Dr. Ward of Newark, New Jersey and Dr. Nicholas of New York, who were pressed into service immediately. Their treatments were a huge mustard plaster on his stomach and chest, some camphor, brandy and water and paragoric. He did not rally, however, for a long time.

A steady stream of anxious people gathered in the hotel and filled the staircase leading to Courtney's room, but only a few were admitted to his room, one of them being Riley. When he saw his big, muscular opponent writhing in pain, Riley said, "The man is sick, and I will not row him. I want a well man to row with, and we will postpone it until Monday or later."

Then Riley went downstairs, where he was met by some of his friends and backers. One of them, Oliver Johnson, in a loud-mouthed manner, said, "Let the sucker come down and row you," going on to say that Courtney's sickness was a sham, a way of getting out of the race, just as he had avoided a race a few years earlier in Philadelphia against Theron Parsons by damaging his paper boat. Arguments continued among Riley's backers and then with the referee, Frank Brown, who finally settled the issue by stating that the race would be rowed at 6:30.

This announcement was made at 6 o'clock, just as Courtney was awakening from his stupor. When he heard it, he tried to get out of bed, saying he wanted to row, but he fell back, exhausted, on the bed. Dr. Olcott told him he positively could not row.

At 6:30 Riley, followed by the crowds, walked to the water and entered his boat. Before the judges started the race, Dr. Olcott stood on the wharf and announced to the crowds, "As Courtney's physician, I am compelled to announce that he is sick and will not be able to take part in the race."

The judges asked Riley if he wanted to row on time, to which he said he did. He went over the course amid cheers from the crowd, making the three miles in 20 minutes 47½ seconds, at the final reckoning, after the timekeeper admitted an inadvertent mistake that would have added a minute to the total time.

Courtney was put on a special railroad car to go to Newark where he stayed for five days at the home of a friend to recover. His boat was put "on the cars," meaning the railroad cars, and sent to Union Springs.

Courtney's backers and caretakers were sharply criticized for being careless, for not guarding him and his equipment closely enough. The Auburn newspaper reporter wrote:

> Had the same care been taken with Courtney that there was with Riley we should no doubt chronicle a very different termination of the contest. Riley put up across the lake in a quiet place, his boat cared for, and food daily brought from New York, and his backers had all the detail well arranged. On the contrary, Courtney was, on the day of the race at this noisy shanty hotel, which was filled with excited people, his food not watched, his boat lying in the sun on a piazza, and his sculls lying in a room filled with the crowd, all exposed to being tampered with, until a friend suggested the sculls be carried upstairs and the boat put in the shade and guarded.

Because there was just one starter in the race, all bets except time bets were off. Courtney had been expected to win, because he had been in superb condition that morning, and he was considered a better oarsman than Riley. Right away his friends offered to back him against Riley at any time for from $1,000 to $10,000.

There was little doubt that Courtney had been dosed with some kind of drug, but it worked too rapidly. It was intended to affect him when he was in his boat on the race course that afternoon, the newspapers reported. "His symptoms were those that would have been produced by tartar emetic, which is much favored by swindling horsemen," the papers said.

Some of Courtney's friends said they had saved a portion of the iced tea and would have it analyzed. Mr. George would say nothing except he was sorry it happened at his hotel. The Greenwood Lake Sportsmen's Club sent a statement to the *New York Times* denying that Mr. George had had anything to do with drugging Courtney, but the *Times* even more strongly stood by its reports.

The plot to drug Courtney evidently had been extensively

known and widely operated on, according to the *New York Times.* They cited the action at the Hoboken pool rooms where the betting on the race was rather even at first, Courtney generally leading in the ratio of one hundred to eighty or ninety. Within an hour or two of race time Riley became a prime favorite and as high as two to one was wagered that he would win. "Among the 'inner circles' of the betting fraternity the feeling was general that Courtney was bound to be defeated by some means—fair if possible, foul if necessary, and the result, therefore, surprised no one," the paper said.

When Courtney returned to Union Springs five days later, he was still feeling weak. However, he reiterated his desire to race Riley on Owasco Lake, the lake east of Cayuga Lake and the site of Auburn, so that more of his "home county" friends could see him race.

During the next week, Courtney signed an affidavit stating that any implications that he sold the race at Greenwood to Riley, that he was afraid to row against Riley and that he feigned sickness, were absolutely false.

In an interview that week with the Auburn paper, which printed the affidavit, he said he was upset by the animus in reports in the *Rochester Express.* But he was amused by the paper's statement that he was afraid to row Theron Parsons of Rochester in Philadelphia. At that time, several years earlier, Parsons was considered only a third or fourth rate oarsman and Courtney could tow him faster than he had ever rowed. Courtney's boat that was slashed to pieces when hit by a practicing oarsman was a paper structure and could not be repaired "as good as ever."

The newspapers continued to hash and rehash the issues of the Greenwood race and the poisoning. The bitterness and the reports fed to the papers by the Neptune Boat Club, where Riley was a member, greatly disturbed Courtney. But he met Riley in competition again that summer and fall.

Cornell Archives

Charles Courtney in his early thirties.

CHAPTER 6

RILEY, AGAIN AND AGAIN

"Courtney Wins; No Poison This Time."

This was the headline in the Ithaca newspaper the evening of the Saratoga Regatta on August 28, 1877. Courtney had rowed in the single scull race of three miles with turn against Riley, his erstwhile antagonist, and Frederick Plaisted of New York and had won by three lengths in 20 minutes 47¾ seconds. Riley was second. The prize was $500, added to the three entrance fees of $100 each, and the championship of America.

Briefly, the paper reported the contest as follows:

> The race started at 11:30 in the morning, all three men settling down to 36 strokes a minute. Courtney passed the half mile leading the others. Plaisted locked oars twice with Riley. They reached the turning points nearly together, Courtney seeming fresh and cool. Riley got on the return course first. Before reaching the half mile on the return, Plaisted gave up, but when the referee's boat reached him, he declined assistance.
>
> Courtney and Riley kept on, Courtney getting a short lead after passing the two-mile stake, which he kept to the end with thirty-four strokes. At the finish he was three lengths ahead of Riley and landed seemingly free from fatigue.
>
> Riley protested, being fouled by Plaisted, but the referee, Mr. Curtis of Chicago, gave the race to Courtney as not being blamable for Plaisted's getting out of his course.

The large crowd of spectators cheered. Some wealthy people expressed a desire to see Courtney and Riley row again, offering to put up several hundred dollars for a purse.

A month later, on September 27, 1877, Courtney rowed against Riley, Nicholas Labergne of Pittsburgh, Pennsylvania and Frenchy Johnson of Boston on Owasco Lake, thus fulfilling his desire to race near home so that many of his neighbors could see him row against other leading oarsmen.

It was a big day for Cayuga County. The schools and businesses of Auburn were closed so everyone could see this race, arranged by George Clark of Ensenore. A grandstand, seating 3,000 people, had been built on a bluff overlooking the lake. An 80–car special train brought more people to the race. An estimated 20,000 people lined the shore. The *Lady of the Lake* steamer and private boats were filled with spectators. The usual peddlers of souvenirs and food were present, as well as the gamblers.

Courtney won easily in his paper boat, said to weigh 31 pounds and measure 29 feet long and 11½ inches wide. The prize was $300. His time in the three-mile race was 21 minutes 29½ seconds.

On October 17 of the same year, Courtney again faced Riley in a sculling race at Owego, New York on the Susquehanna River. Before the professional oarsmen raced, the amateurs tested their abilities against each other. One of the amateurs that day was Courtney's nephew, 19–year-old Robert Larmon of Union Springs. Larmon, one of the young men Courtney was training at the Springs, won the singles race and received the prize, a silver water set. The course was two miles with turn.

Undoubtedly Courtney was proud of his nephew, one of many young men he helped to become good oarsmen. Courtney was earning a living at the planing mill he and his brother John operated, and in the rowing season he entered many competitions, but in his spare time he enjoyed helping the young men who practiced on the lake or exercised in his workshop.

Besides Courtney and Riley in the professional single sculling race, there was Frenchy Johnson. The race was three miles with turn. Courtney led from the start, winning the race with the time of 20 minutes 14¾ seconds, said to be the best time for three miles on record at that time. Riley was three quarters of a boat length behind and Johnson several lengths behind him. The prizes were $200, $150 and $75.

For this race Courtney wore the blue neckerchief he had worn fifty-seven times before when he was victorious in three-mile races.

The *Ithaca Journal* printed some accounts from the *Binghamton Times* in which a reporter described each of the professional contestants and related some conversations with them before the race. He called Courtney the champion sculler of the world and said he was 29 years old, six feet one-half inches tall and weighed 185 pounds dressed, but 180 pounds as he rowed. His chest measurement was 42½ inches. "He has a large frame, rather deep set eyes with heavy black eyebrows and hair, and a well-modeled face with regular features," the account said.

After reviewing Courtney's early life, carpentry business and early rowing career, the account states:

> He was, as he expressed it, feeling perfectly well, though now down where he ought to be if hard pushed in the race. He seemed to feel the utmost confidence, however, and while not evincing the least disposition to boast, he remarked in a quiet manner, such as to inspire entire confidence, that he meant what he said: "I guess I can row fast enough." He spoke in terms of praise of both his competitors and predicted the fastest time on record. . . . The only fault Courtney finds with anything or anybody, and that was only elicited by questioning, was that at the outset he had a hard row to hoe against the press, more particularly of New York City, but that now when victory perched upon his banners they were all right enough. He had been solicited by New York papers on several occasions to write explanatory articles concerning races rowed, and others talked of but not rowed, but has preferred to remain silent and fight his battles with the blades and in his boat, and make his record in that way. Newspapers' puffings, he says, "don't get you over the line first." . . . One characteristic of Courtney is that he never bet a dollar on a boat race in his life. . . . He came to Owego on a kind of picnic on this trip, he says, and has been shooting considerable; he is a good shot, and bagged eight partridges on Tuesday.
>
> Courtney rowed in a paper boat, 29 feet in length, 11½ inches wide, weighing 31 pounds, sliding seat and using sculls nine feet eight inches long. The boat was built by Waters and Son of Troy.

Riley was the next to be described and interviewed. Also

29 years old, Riley is a farmer in his hometown of Saratoga, the account said. He answered all questions in a pleasant, unostentatious manner and said that he has been rowing in public about four years. The reporter described him as follows:

> He is six feet in height and weighs, with clothes on, 159 pounds. Has dark hair, light black side whiskers and moustache, and as his weight indicates, is rather lightly built, but there is not an ounce of superfluous flesh on his body. He is browned by exposure, has a wiry, tough look, and is, in fact, in appearance, "as fine as silk." He said he felt pretty well, although troubled with a slight cough, but should have no excuses if beaten. In manner and conversation he is a gentleman, and in no sense manifests a boastful disposition. He has rowed some eighteen or twenty races in public in all, and has never been defeated except by Courtney. He is a coming man and will prove a tough customer for the best.
>
> His boat is a paper one, and the exact counterpart of Courtney's being 29 feet long, 11½ inches wide and weighing 31 pounds.

"Frenchy A. Johnson," the reporter wrote, "is not, as his name might be supposed to indicate, at all Frenchy either in nationality or nature, but is a native of Virginia, having formerly been a slave." The account continues:

> He was born at Germantown, Virginia, is 27 years of age, weighs 163 pounds and is about 5 feet 8½ inches in height. He now resides in Boston where his first rowing was done a year ago last June on the Charles River, winning second money. He also rowed on Silver Lake, near Boston, again winning second money; and in the fourth of July regatta of this year, at Boston. He seems well-educated and conducts himself in a becoming and gentlemanly manner.

Frenchy Johnson became a close associate and helper, sometimes referred to as a trainer, of Courtney within the next two years of his professional rowing career. Riley continued to row in professional races.

All these encounters with Riley undoubtedly influenced the naming of the Courtneys' family cat. It seems that a beautiful, big tiger cat was sent to Courtney from Saratoga and immediately preferred him to the rest of the family. One day he found the cat on his bed when he returned home. He picked it up and took it downstairs where some guests were in the parlor. "What shall I do with it? It won't leave my room?" he asked the visitors.

"You must not part with him. Your luck will go also if you do," one of the guests said.

"It isn't luck that makes me win. It's hard practice and tight living," Courtney replied.

One of the women put a big, scarlet ribbon on the cat's neck, saying "Bring Mr. Courtney luck, kitty."

"His name shall be 'Jim.' Come on, Jim Riley," Courtney laughed, and let the cat follow him wherever he could. The cat lived many years with the family, but was always known at home and in the neighborhood as "Charlie's cat."

Cayuga County Historical Society

Charles Courtney in 1878 in his racing costume, which included the shirt with the blue star on it.

CHAPTER 7

COURTNEY AND HANLAN

"The first time I was beaten was by Hanlan, at Lachine, in 1878. You will find plenty of men who will tell you I crossed the line first; I always had my opinion in the matter, but the race was awarded to him, and I accepted the decision of the judges. I had no business to be racing any longer at that time, anyway. Man isn't a steam engine; you can't go on shoveling in coal all the time. The time will come, as I said before, when nature will assert itself," Courtney told Professor W. T. Hewett, author of the 1905 *History of Cornell University.*

"Then [after the Lachine race] great efforts were made to have us meet again; but the way the newspapers pitched into me, and the outrageous falsehoods that they circulated, caused me to become indifferent about it. I was even accused of cowardice," Courtney continued.

"I had rowed in eighty-eight contests and won every time, and now that I was beaten once, the American public seemed to lose its head. I was beaten by one of the best oarsmen that ever sat in a boat. And I know this—that there was but precious little difference between us two," Courtney declared.

This was Courtney's assessment in retrospect of one of the most disappointing and frustrating episodes in his racing career. Edward Hanlan of Toronto had gained immediate international attention when he won the professional single sculling race at the International Regatta in Philadelphia in 1876 in the record time of 21 minutes 9½ seconds. Courtney gained just as much attention because he won the amateur prize at the same regatta but not in outstanding time. In August 1877, however, Courtney, who was then a professional, rowed over the same course as Hanlan had the year before and broke

Hanlan's record by more than 20 seconds.

Now there was a great public clamor for the two oarsmen to face each other. The possibilities for monetary gain by the auxiliary enterprises—hotel keepers, railroads, salemen of souvenirs and gamblers—far exceeded the prizes for the participants. The big question was: Where would they race?

Commenting on the situation on September 8, 1878, The *Ithaca Journal* said: "It requires a careful thinker to keep posted in regard to these two renowned diplomat-oarsmen. One day the contest is to be at this place and in this manner, another day we are told it is to be that way and at that place, and soon we may expect to hear that the whole thing has proved a battle of words."

The battle for the site of the race was between the Americans who wanted it on Owasco Lake and the Canadians, represented by the Toronto Rowing Club, who wanted it at Toronto. One proposal from the Canadians said that Hanlan would row on Owasco only if Courtney would row him at Toronto. The editors at Ithaca and Auburn were outraged at the demands of Hanlan and his backers, who wanted to receive, as conditions of the race agreemnt, large percentages of the receipts taken by the Southern Central Railroad and all other enterprises from the day Hanlan arrived. As much as they wanted the race on Owasco Lake, the editors said they would not blame Courtney and his backers if they turned down this proposal, which they did.

After much haggling, the five-mile race with a turn was scheduled for October 3, 1878 on the St. Lawrence River at Lachine, near Montreal, Quebec. The prize was $11,000 with $6,000 of it from Montreal and $2,500 from the supporters of each contestant.

This race between Hanlan and Courtney, as well as the two that followed, received more publicity throughout the world than any other sporting event up to 1880, the *Ontario History* said. Rowing was the fashionable sport in the late 1870s, as well as a very profitable one for the gamblers. Both men had been rowing and winning regularly, although Hanlan had appeared in more races than Courtney.

Newspapers on both sides of the border noted every aspect of the careers of the two men, and fairly or not, brought up anything that might be detrimental to the other nation's oarsman. The Canadians called Courtney overrated and then cited his mishaps, such as the poisoning at Greenwood Lake, insinuating that he may have been pretending to be drugged. They cited his smashed paper boat at Philadelphia, when he was hit by a practicing oarsman, as something he did on purpose. And they recalled that he had turned over once on Seneca Lake, claiming that a wire had been placed beneath the water, catching his oar and overturning the boat, but no wire was found.

The American papers had ammunition, too. They recalled that in a July Fourth race in 1877 at Boston, Hanlan had been ruled out for fouling Fred Plaisted whom he ran into at the turning stake. The officials of the regatta, sponsored by the Citizens Association, were so offended by Hanlan's conduct that they passed a resolution recommending that he be barred from participating in all races under municipal management. Hanlan appealed the decision, and eventually, through efforts of his backers, the bar against him was removed.

The American press said that Hanlan's father, who had died earlier, had a saloon on the island in Toronto Bay where the family lived, and from here he carried on a surreptitious traffic in drinkables. The saloon was operated then by Hanlan's brother. His mother, a hale and hearty Irishwoman, was still alive. His sister was also skillful at rowing and reportedly sat with all the grace of her famous brother in a shell. The Hanlan Club, his backers, made sure that their oarsman did not have to work, but had plenty of time to practice, according to American news accounts.

Hanlan, a handsome, dark-haired young man, was greatly admired by women. And he often put on a good show during the races, pretending to be sick and then suddenly straightening up and rowing to the fore. Or he would wave to bystanders. He could do this because he often put on a spurt of power at the start of a race, gaining a good lead, and then he rowed the remainder almost leisurely. Spectators were awed by his rowing power, since he was rather slight, compared with his competitors.

William Blaikie, a celebrated Harvard oarsman and New York City attorney who occasionally was a referee at sculling races, was interviewed by the *Ithaca Journal* about three weeks before the race.

"I can't quite understand it," he said. "It is very curious that the race is not for the championship. Then, too, the prize is enormous—$11,000. I don't believe there was ever such a stake rowed for in this country before."

When asked if he thought it would be a fair race, he replied," I believe the men intend to row fairly. I have always had faith in Courtney. He is a splendid fellow, just what he is, a farmer's son, strong, healthy, and full of confidence in himself. He has often told me that he is not afraid to row any man in the world."

"Can he beat Hanlan?" the reporter asked.

"Physically, he ought to be able to, but I doubt whether he trains properly. Hanlan has improved his 'wind' wonderfully by running nine miles every day. Courtney does not believe in running, and I am inclined to think that he is a very much better man than Hanlan; he may be beaten over a long course just because he has failed to take that precaution."

After the reporter suggested Courtney should be careful because he has had several mishaps, Blaikie said, "They have hurt his reputation. I believe him to be a square man, but there is a great deal of talk about him . . . many ill-natured remarks.

"I am inclined to think he has got into bad hands," Blaikie continued. "He is a simple, inexperienced fellow, and no match for professional sharpers. He is not his own man. He has let men get influence over him by providing him with board and so on. He ought to pay anything that he owes in that way, and say plainly that he is going to consult his own interests and reputation and not other persons. Hanlan has already beaten him in a financial sense."

"How's that?"

"Well," he said to Courtney at the beginning of the season,

'Look here, Charlie, I don't want to row you now, because if you beat me, my backers won't support me in matches with second rate men, and if I beat you, I shan't be able to get anyone to row against me. Let us put off our match until late in the season.' Courtney consented, and while Hanlan has been winning race after race, he has done nothing at all. So Hanlan occupies the best position. He has kept himself before the public, has been ready to row anybody who came along, and has fairly won the title of champion."

As to the Lachine course, Blaikie said, "I understand there is a wide current there, which is rather troublesome. On a former occasion they tried to neutralize the effect of it by anchoring a long line of barges outside the course. Hanlan knows the course better than Courtney, and that is to his advantage, but, of course, Courtney will go there at once to practice, and it won't take him long to learn."

The editor commented on Blaikie's statements, saying that, as regards the relative rowing ability of the two men, his observations are considered as nearly accurate because they are based on his careful observations. But, as regards Courtney having fallen into bad hands, however, "we think Mr. Blaikie is in error."

The Canadians reported that as the day of the race approached, the interest in it intensified. Telegrams came in from all over the United States, England and Europe, requesting information about the race and the oarsmen. The betting favored Hanlan.

On race day, the weather was not promising. The water was rough and the wind strong. By one o'clock, condititons had improved and it was anounced that the race would be rowed at 2:30. The referee, Sheriff Harding of St. John, New Brunswick, went on board the steamer *Gatinean,* which then went over the course to inspect the buoys. One of them had drifted about 100 feet and had to be put back in place. The buoys were about 200 feet apart and each man had to turn from the left to the right, according to the articles of the race agreement. To prevent trouble, a man was sent out to adjust the turning buoys and was told to stay there until the rowers passed.

On the steamer, men representing Hanlan and Courtney drew for position. Hanlan won the right to choose, and he picked the outside lane to the south, thereby getting in the lee of Isle Dorval, the largest island on the course.

Before the steamer left the buoys, storm clouds were gathering. Lightning flashed and thunder rolled. A pouring rain began, and the officials on the steamer questioned the advisability of having the race. But by the time the steamer got to the starting point, the storm had passed, and the sun came out. So, the race was on.

In the meantime, train after train had brought in an estimated 20,000 visitors. Flags were flying at the quarters of the contestants, vendors followed the crowds to the shoreline and to every vantage point along the river. After the storm and other delays, at 4:15 the steamer finally gave four whistles, the signal for the contestants to appear.

Hanlan was the first to come to the starting point. He wore a blue shirt with red trimming, and a red cap. He was followed by Courtney who had on a white shirt with the blue star in the front and a sky blue cap. Both men had heavy, dark mustaches, popular in that era.

They dipped sculls together, Hanlan pulling 31 strokes a minute and Courtney 38. The lead, always slim, changed several times, with the pace seeming to get faster and faster, as the two shells sped "fairly hissing through the water." The cheers from the spectators were deafening.

There are several versions of what happened as the men reached the last two thirds of a mile of the course. One account said that Hanlan spurted ahead by three boat lengths, then Courtney pulled harder and faster and kept gaining on Hanlan. There was still time for Courtney to win, but some obstacles, said to be barges, had drifted into the lanes. Both oarsmen had to change course to avoid them. Hanlan paused and Courtney paused, too, but longer. Hence Hanlan won the race by a boat length and a quarter. Another account said that Courtney slowed down noticeably after the first 2½ miles and Hanlan won easily.

In an article about Courtney in *The Oarsman* of July-August

Cornell Archives

Edward Hanlan of Toronto, Canadian champion and International Professional champion in 1876.

1978, Thomas C. Mendenhall, a present day authority on rowing, wrote:

> Hanlan could not shake the determined Courtney who never let him get more than two lengths ahead despite the wind, tide and rough water. Only a length back at the turn, Courtney drew level at the final mile, with both scullers at 32. Some boats had come inside the booms at the finish. Hanlan worked his way through them first, to win by a length and a half. The confusion at the finish, together with the fact that the odds over Hanlan had markedly increased just before the start, made the outcome suspect and fed the fires for a return match.

The Ithaca paper reported on the day after the race:

> The general belief here is that Courtney sold yesterday's race. The *Tribune*'s Montreal special says there were some things about the race which certainly give color to suspicion, such as Courtney's poor rowing in the last mile when his stroke never exceeded 32, and the very crooked steering of both men near the finish, Courtney getting very much into Hanlan's water and having to

> stop short just before reaching the line to avoid a foul. At any rate, whether it is true or not, many people hold the opinion very firmly that the result has already hurt Courtney's reputation, and will do much to throw professional rowing into disfavor. It is however impossible to tell whether the race was honestly rowed or not, and 'til Courtney can be asked to explain things which seem suspicious now it is not fair to prejudge him, nor can there be any question that it was an uncommonly pretty race to look at and one in which the men seemed to be very evenly matched.

The following day the Ithaca paper carried an account of interviews with both scullers:

> The *Herald*'s Montreal dispatch reports an interview with Hanlan and Courtney. Hanlan declared the race was fair, that Courtney gave him the hardest work he ever had to win, and he was the first rower that he (Hanlan) could not do with as he pleased. Hanlan says he won just nine dollars which he bet with Courtney's cook, but had heard that Courtney lost several hundred which he (Courtney) bet on himself. Hanlan added, if Courtney challenged him, he would be oblidged to accept and believes he can beat Courtney every time.
>
> Courtney stated he felt very bad over the cruel charge made against him, and but for that he would immediately challenge Hanlan to row again. He declared the rough water defeated him, and that Hanlan's choice of the outside course made a difference of a minute on the first mile; also that he was delayed at the turning buoys, it having been stated that his buoy would be marked by the American flag while in fact both flags were displayed. As to the finish, Courtney declared the current took both rowers out of their courses.

The debate over the fairness of the race, the possibility of foul play and the chance that it may have been "sold" continued in both countries. Courtney had said on several earlier occasions that he never bet on the races. He had many friends who attested to his integrity. One thing seemed sure: Courtney and Hanlan would meet again.

CHAPTER 8

THE CHAUTAUQUA LAKE FIZZLE

The race between Courtney and Hanlan at Lachine was talked about in the saloons, clubs, drawing rooms and on the streets of the United States and Canada for many months. The interest of the citizens was fanned by the daily newspapers, which ran in-depth stories criticizing the race, the fairness of it in view of the currents in the water and the obstacles that drifted into the race course. Some papers claimed that Courtney actually won.

The newspapers accused each other of errors in reporting, in particular the *Auburn Daily Advertiser* of Auburn, New York, which criticized the gross errors of the *New York Herald* in giving the incorrect dates and times of some of Courtney's races. The Auburn paper had a memorandum of all Courtney's time in all his principal races, "the information coming from his own lips," the paper said. The Lachine race was referred to as "the great fight with Hanlan." More and more newspapers urged a rematch of the two oarsmen, saying that the sporting world and the ordinary citiizens were demanding it.

Courtney was anxious, the papers said, to race Hanlan again to clear his name of the rumor that he had sold the race, but he wanted less turbulent waters than those at Lachine.

Finally Asa T. Soule, president of the Hop Bitters Company of Rochester, New York, makers of the patent medicine, "The Invalid's Friend and Hope," offered a purse of $6,000 for a five-mile race with turn on Chautauqua Lake, in southwestern New York, to be rowed on October 8, 1879. The articles of agreement were signed in Rochester by Courtney on September 12. Hanlan signed soon afterward in Toronto. The race was to be for the prize of $6,000, not for the championship.

Immediately the press billed the contest as "the race of the century."

Chautauqua Lake was chosen because it was neutral water, meaning it had "never felt the touch of either Courtney's or Hanlan's keel," the *Daily Journal* of Jamestown, New York reported. Also, the lake was "centrally located and connected with the outside world by four lines of railroads going to all points of the compass." About seventy miles south of Buffalo, the lake was popular summer resort, with plenty of accomodations at the large hotels. The many steamships that plied the lake waters would be available to spectators. The lake was convenient for the Canadians and would also draw people from Pittsburgh, Cleveland and even Chicago, which would send a train to pick up spectators on its way east. A steamer on Lake Erie would take spectators from Canada to Dunkirk on the American side, in Chautauqua County, where they could get a train to the lake.

Often the weather was favorable in October on Chautauqua Lake, which stretches from Mayville southeasterly to Jamestown, a distance of about twenty miles. The race was to be rowed at the northern end, near Mayville, with the start and finish opposite Fair Point, the site of present day Chautauqua Institution, the world-famous religious and cultural summer community. In those days it was called the Chautauqua Assembly and was just emerging from its beginnings as a Methodist Camp Meeting Ground.

In an effort to guarantee an error-proof race, the articles of the agreement covered many details, at the insistence of William Blaikie, who had been chosen referee. The race was to be governed by the rules of the National Association of Amateur Oarsmen. The contestants were to toss for positions and were to start from two boats moored twenty-five yards apart and row two and a half miles to buoys securely anchored and properly marked with flags. Each man was to run his buoy from port to starboard. A line of flags was to be placed between the two lanes. An official survey of the course was to be made by engineers.

The race was to be between three and six o'clock in the

afternoon on smooth water. The referee was empowered to postpone the race to the next day or to the first favorable day. Also, he could order the men to row again on the first favorable day if any outside interference affected the result of the race. This point of the agreement was a touchy issue in the final outcome.

Soule originally put up $5,000 for the race with the plan that it be for the championship and open to all who wanted to compete. Both Courtney and Hanlan declined to row in such a race. Then Soule offered $6,000 in prize money to go to the winner of a race between the two men and them only on American waters, agreed upon by both parties.

As soon as word of the upcoming race was received, the small communities along Chautauqua Lake were humming with activity, especially Mayville, the county seat and the town nearest to the race course. Resort hotels, which had ended their official summer season, were again booked full several weeks ahead of time. Private homes owners were booking the overflow of visitors. Gambling men began to arrive and started selling odds at the local saloons and hotels, or any place they could.

Carpenters were busy erecting the grandstand that faced the start and finish line and had a lake frontage of 2,000 feet. On the other three sides of the grandstand, high board fences were being built to make an enclosure for refreshment stands.

Railway workers were laying a spur of the railroad that would follow the race course and would end at the grandstand. Observation cars were being prepared to carry spectators along this route. This spur was variously called the Hop Bitters Railway or the Prospect Railway. One man suggested it be called the Bitter Hops.

When the oarsmen arrived late in September to set up their headquarters, the preparations intensified. Reporters from the leading newspapers were on hand and vied for the best interviews with the contestants. Artist from *Harper's Weekly,* the *Daily Graphic* of New York and the *Canadian Illustrated News* were there. In the Jamestown paper there was a long, daily account of the activites, under the heading, "The Race."

Hanlan arrived at Chautauqua Lake on September 23, coming from Toronto where he lived with his wife and young daughter. The following day the papers reported that he was in poor health and was seeking a postponement. He stayed at hotels near the lake, first at the Mayville House in Mayville, then moved to the Pickard House at Bemus Point, halfway down the lake toward Jamestown, and finally returned to Mayville, staying at the Chautauqua House. He had several trainers with him.

Hanlan brought three shells with him, all made by G. and J. Wharin of Toronto. His racing shell was named *Louise* in honor of Princess Louise, Queen Victoria's daughter. Patterned after an English model, this shell was made of white cedar, was 31 feet long, 11 inches wide amidships and 5 inches deep at that spot. It weighed less than 30 pounds with outriggers.

When talking about the $6,000 prize, Hanlan joked that he "wouldn't like to get the bitter end of it," and added that he intended to give the race his utmost effort.

In a more serious vein, Hanlan gave a statement to the Jamestown paper that reflects some of the pressure from the public:

> I know what losing means. It means that I need never set my foot in Toronto again. I could get money enough to live off all my days if I rowed crooked, but while I can row a race I will row to win. People will be on me if I start at all, no matter in what condition I am in, and no matter how I tell them I feel. Such people will say, if I lose, that what I say about myself is to let myself down easy, and so I will be hounded the way Courtney was. I have got a wife and child, and I don't like the prospect, so I am going to win. The purse is good, and I'm going to have it.

Courtney arrived on September 24 on a special railway car from Rochester, bringing one shell, his trainer Frenchy Johnson, (the man he had rowed against at Owego) and several other associates. He stayed at the residence of John W. Cornell, a mile and a half from Mayville toward Fair Point and the Chautauqua Assembly.

Courtney's racing shell, named *Hop Bitters* in honor of Soule's company, arrived on October 2, wrapped in canvas and suspended from the ceiling of a railway car. It was 31 feet long,

Photo by the author

This house, formerly the John W. Cornell family homestead, now owned by Catherine Ten Eyck, near Mayville on Chautauqua Lake, is where Courtney stayed in 1879 while training for the race with Hanlan that fall.

11½ inches wide amidships and 5¾ inches deep at that spot. At the stern it was 3 inches deep and 4½ inches deep at the bow. It weighed 27 pounds with outriggers, and had been made by E. Waters and Sons of Troy, New York, makers of paper boats. "Mr. Waters says it is the finest boat in the world," the Jamestown paper reported.

When Courtney arrived at Chautauqua Lake he heard that Hanlan had already asked for a postponement to October 16 because of illness and it had been granted. Courtney sent one of his backers, James Brister of Auburn, to Toronto to protest the postponement, but to no avail. The race would be on the 16th.

A conversation between Blaikie and Courtney was reported in the Ithaca paper:

"You will have to work hard, Courtney," said Blaikie, "for Hanlan just told me that he is going to row for everything there is in him."

"I should think he would," replied Courtney, laughing, "for $6,000. But he won't be the only one working hard. It is not always that a man has a chance to earn as much money in one day as that."

The prize, indeed, was quite a lot of money in 1879, when the costs of other things are considered. The rowing shells costs about $125 to $150, butter was 10¢ a pound, a pair of blankets was $1.50, chemises with embroidery and ruffles were 80¢, waitresses at the best hotels earned $21 a month, the Harvey Houses paid $1.50 for a dozen prairie chickens and 75¢ for a dozen quail to cook for their guests, and the $5,000 annual salary for the head chef at the Palmer House in Chicago was considered outrageously high.

On October 1, Hanlan's racing shell was damaged while it was being launched, being crushed against a float and suffering a jagged hole in its side. Hanlan took the accident "calmly" and immediately made arrangements to get a new boat from the Wharin firm, who made all his boats with the same dimensions.

Watching the oarsmen practice was a very popular diversion for the people who lived along the lake or who were arriving for the big event. The steamboats ran special excursions from Jamestown to the north end of the lake to watch the oarsmen. Private boats were filled with sightseers. Newspapers gave regular accounts of the contestants' activities, reporting on how they looked and what they ate.

Hanlan was described as having a "magnificent physical appearance" being slight but muscular and weighing 155 pounds. Then his body measurements were given. "He eats substantially good food, but no pastry. He takes a bottle of Bass Pale Ale with his meals," one account said. He took regular walks, covering ten miles a day and two pulls in his boat. "His backers coddle his spirit as much as his body," the reporter wrote.

As for Courtney, the paper said that, being somewhat sequestered from the public view by the retired location of his quarters, he is not so well known to the public as Mr. Hanlan.

He is satisfied with the fare except for the water, which is impalatable. He never partakes of wine, spirits or malt liquor. He takes long walks every day, often nearly to Lake Erie, at least to where he can see the water. He takes two vigorous pulls in his boat. The reporter got his weight—170 pounds, and his height—6′ ½″, but when he asked Courtney for his measurements, the oarsman replied, "No man puts a tape measure to me except my tailor." The sightseers who went on Sundays to see Courtney row were disappointed; he did not row on Sundays.

As the race day approached, betting reached a fever pitch. "Every game of chance and skill, from that which is played 'on the square' to the most base are in full blast. Private houses are turned into dens where a most ferocious 'tiger is bucked' and no locality seems to be free from the presences of the crookeds," one newsman noted.

The gambling men and all the hundreds who were there to make a quick dollar, did not appeal to the local gentry. "Sporting men, with their immense chains, seal rings and pins, such as no civilized humans were outside the sporting fraternity" filled Mayville and its environs, reaching to Chautauqua Assembly Grounds. All church-going residents were upset by this avalanche of sin that had overtaken them.

Among the people who had come for the race was Soule, who was described as "about 50 with long, dark hair, a white beard and clothed in a solemn black broadcloth. He looks like a Methodist minister with a revival on his mind, and one might ask him when the meeting begins, but the question would be malapropos, as he is not what his looks portend."

Vendors were selling pictures of Hanlan and Courtney, ties bearing their colors, and every imaginable gimmick that promoted these two men whose "names are on every tongue." Hanlan's group promoted handsome silk handkerchiefs with the initials E. R. in the center, surrounded by the crests of England, Canada and the United States. In each corner there was a representation of the Canadian beaver. The border was red and white.

The boathouses of the oarsmen drew a great deal of attention. At Courtney's an American flag flew overhead. Some accounts say that as the race day approached, he hired several men to take turns staying there as sentinels. Hanlan's boathouse was surrounded by a high board fence to keep off the curious crowds. Hanlan visited Courtney's boathouse twice, but Courtney never visited Hanlan's.

The day before the race, a telegraph line was installed between the grandstand and the Western Union office. It was announced that the steam yacht *Waukeegan* would be the referee boat. The Mayville dock had been converted into a beer garden where vendors of the "lager and sandwich" were doing a thriving business with promise of an increase. Some people were still constructing booths of wood and canvas where they prepared to sell anything they could. "The intoxicating liquor and solid, sallow sandwich will be easy to procure," the Jamestown reporter wrote.

The pool-selling was controlled by Quimby and Forse, well-known New York pool-operators, who were doing business in the billiard room of the Chautauqua House the night before the race. Hanlan was favored slightly, but, as the Jamestown reporter pointed out, most of those buying in favor of Hanlan in the pools were Canadians. Among the Canadians were members of the Hanlan Club, Messrs. Davis, Shaw, Ward and McConnell.

At his boathouse, Courtney watched Frenchy put a mirror-like gloss on the racing shell. Hanlan claimed to be under the weather. Blaikie visited both boathouses to inform the men that the hour would be four o'clock, and later said that Hanlan seemed to be improved.

Even though all the hotels and boardinghouses were full, people continued to arrive and were willing to sleep anywhere—on chairs, tables or the floor. Lacking beds, people rented dry goods crates for a quarter a night, piano boxes for a half a dollar, and farmers sold hay for bedding.

The crowds were sensitive to any indication about the outcome of the race. Any omen was taken seriously, therefore Courtney's success was predicted when it was learned that two

Chautauqua County Historical Society

These are samples of the tickets for the steamer, the grandstand and the enclosure at the 1879 race on Chautauqua Lake between Courtney and Hanlan.

dogs at the Cornell residence had taken a liking to him and slept under his bed.

The night before the race, the speculation mounted, the betting grew brisker, and few people in Mayville slept. "The all important object among sporting and news men is to 'get a point'—'scent a job'—but so far as I can learn no one has been able to detect a sign that the race has been 'fixed,' " a Jamestown reporter wrote for the morning edition the day of the race.

The morning of the 16th found Jamestown almost a ghost town, because everyone was on his way to the northern end of the lake. The air was clear, cool and pleasantly sunny after an early morning fog lifted. For a week it had been unusually warm for October, so warm, in fact, that Courtney had decided to wear his cap as protection against the sun instead of his blue handkerchief on his head. If this day turned out like the several days before it, the surface of the lake would be as still as a mirror at the end of the day. Both Courtney and Hanlan had expressed their pleasure at having the race here. The number of people who had come to the lake to see the "race of the century" had been estimated at 25,000 the night before.

Storekeepers were just opening their doors, and the hotel kitchens were getting breakfasts ready, when the rumor spread that during the night Courtney's boats had been sawed in two.

Speculation was rampant. Who sawed the boats? Would the race be rowed? What of the bets that had been made? Mayville was in an uproar.

When two Jamestown reporters went to Courtney's headquarters at the Cornell residence, Courtney said, "Boys, they sawed my boats in two. Then he explained that he was awakened at 5:30 that morning by Bob Larmon, his nephew, and Burt Brown, both of them amateur oarsmen, who had been hired to help with his boats. These two men had told Courtney that they left the boathouse at 6:00 o'clock the evening before to go to Mayville for supper and on an errand. When they left they locked the boathouse door on the lake side with a padlock and hooked the rear door, then put a nail over the hook. When they returned from Mayville, they found the rear door had been forced, the nail broken, and both boats cut in two. The racing shell was sawed nearly through, in a diagonal direction 12′ 10″ from the bow. The practice shell was sawed entirely through 6′ 4″ from the stern.

They did not tell Courtney, but went to Frenchy Johnson, his trainer, who told them not to disturb Courtney until morning because the oarsman needed his rest. Frenchy Johnson told reporters that Courtney wept like a baby when he went to the boathouse and saw his boats.

Courtney had spent the evening before at Cornells, playing euchre with the hired man, Ed Bartle, and then talking with Mrs. Cornell and her daughter, telling them about some of his rowing experiences. While they were talking, they heard someone outside the house, then heard a foot strike against the side of the house. "Skeets," as Bartle was called, ran to the door and saw a man disappear in the darkness.

When Courtney and his assistants were looking around the boathouse, they found a band saw in the 18 inches of water beneath the boats.

Rumors were spread through the crowds that Courtney had sawed his own boats, that he had asked Frenchy Johnson to do it, that the saw belonged to Frenchy, and that the boathouse had been left unguarded purposely.

The rumor about the saw was discredited in two ways. It later developed that the saw belonged to a confectioner from Rochester who brought it to use in building his booth. Then when Frenchy returned to Union Springs, some citizens demanded to inspect his trunk because they had been told, via the press, that the saw would be found in it. But there was no saw in his trunk.

Courtney asked for a ten-day postponement, the time it would take him to get a new boat from the Waters Company. He said the two damaged shells were the only two of that kind made by the firm according to his own specifications. Courtney felt he was entitled to this postponement in view of the postponement granted earlier to Hanlan because of illness. But Blaikie refused to give him a postponement.

Blaikie went to Courtney's boathouse and quizzed him about the episode. He asked Courtney to row in another boat, either the boat Frenchy had brought with him, or one of Hanlan's. Courtney said Frenchy's boat was too light for him. He refused to accept the use of one of Hanlan's boats because he said he was not used to it and it would place himself at a marked disadvantage.

As race time approached, Blaikie, the judge for Hanlan, members of the press and timekeepers went in the judge's boat to Courtney's boathouse. Blaikie sent word to Courtney that he wanted him to come out and row in one of the boats mentioned before, even at a loss of the race. Courtney absolutely refused to come out, as did his backers. The judge's boat then steamed over to Hanlan's quarters.

Chautauqua County Historical Society

Labeled *The Chautauqua Lake Fizzle,* this drawing appeared in the *Daily Graphic* of New York City on October 17, 1879, the day after the aborted race. The drawing shows Hanlan rowing the course alone, with people watching from the steamers and the shore. Above Hanlan is a drawing of Courtney's racing scull. The map at top shows the location of Mayville, the race course, Fair Point (Now Chautauqua Institution), the grandstand, the Cornell farm where Courtney stayed, the boathouses (quarters) of the two men and the railroad extension.

Hanlan was already on the lake, ready to start. At 4:44 the word "Go" was given and Hanlan started amid the cheers of the crowds, still about 20,000. His stroke ranged from 28 to 36 a minutes, and he reached the turning point in 16 minutes. He often stopped for a few strokes and looked around, and people expected some of his antics, which he often used to delight the crowds when he was well ahead of his opponents. But this day he just wiped his face with his handkerchief. He finished the course in 33 minutes 56¼ seconds. Charles M. Calvin, who acted as judge for Courtney, declared Hanlan the winner of the purse.

Courtney watched Hanlan from the shore and vowed that if Hanlan did not row the course in less than 33 minutes, he (Courtney) could beat him. He said he had rowed over the course in 33 minutes 3 seconds in practice.

The Auburn reporter noted that "the impression is that Courtney is entirely free from suspicion. Hanlan's people undoubtedly tried to put up a job on Courtney, who is only blameable for trusting men about him to look after the boats and management."

The *Troy Times* also scolded Courtney for not insisting that his boats be guarded more carefully, saying, "If Courtney has not seen enough of the racing business to know that it is as necessary to have a guard over his boathouse as it is to have a referee on the trial day, he would do well to stick to his shop henceforth."

The Jamestown paper said:

> Everyone who had been at Courtney's boathouse in the last few days would say it was left unguarded by carelessness, not by design. Brister should have looked after the boats . . . Courtney was left to take care of things himself. Courtney had no motive to destroy his boats. If he thought Hanlan could beat him, he could have easily sold out, rowed a close or losing race in quick time and saved his honor. . . . Facts seem to throw the blame on the Hanlan party who didn't want defeat. All who saw Courtney were impressed with his sincerity and genuine regret.

In answer to people who said Courtney had paid some of his own men to cut his boats, or that he had done it himself so he would not have to row, Courtney replied that he would stake his life on the fact that none of his men ruined his boats.

Courtney declared that this race was the most villainous scheme ever concocted in any country. "I can tell enough about them (the Hanlan group) to fill a dictionary. I am willing to swear to what I say. It has always been our custom to have the boathouses unguarded. We are sorry we did not guard the boathouse, as it was a fatal mistake."

Courtney told reporters that he had told Blaikie the week before about the offers he had received to fix the race. He also said his life had been threatened, and for this reason he had been carrying a gun the last few days. Courtney showed reporters some of the threatening notes he had received. One was signed "Jack and Jill," and the other bore the name "Justess."

One of the agreements that Hanlan's men offered to Courtney was written on the back of a telegraph blank in "a peculiar hand," with a lead pencil. It had been given to Brister by John Davis of Toronto, one of Hanlan's backers, with the statement that unless Courtney signed it, Hanlan would not row the race. It was a statement that the contestants would split the purse. Another of Hanlan's backers, David Ward, promised Courtney half of the money in the pool box, said to be about $100,000, if he would sign the note. Courtney refused to sign the scribbled note. His answer was always a firm "No" to any such offers.

Blaikie was criticized for violating the agreement by letting Hanlan row alone and by not postponing the race. The agreement said that in case of interference, the referee should order the men to row over again on the first favorable day under the original conditions.

The Jamestown paper said:

> By starting Hanlan, Blaikie tacitly declared that Courtney's boats were not sawed by outside parties, a decision he had no right to make on the evidence then in. If he had postponed the race, in accordance with Courtney's request, the public would have had the matter of Courtney's willingness to meet Hanlan decided forever as well as the superiority of one or the other of the oarsmen. A refusal of Courtney's courteous request for postponement came with poor grace from Hanlan who had forced the first postponement.

Although Hanlan rowed the course, Quimby and Forse declared all bets and pools off unless they had been made with the stipulation of "play or pay." Many deals came to light during the next few days. Hop Bitters had a percentage on the pools sold and owned all the privileges sold to the gamblers, several newspaper reported.

Hanlan did not get the $6,000. He received the check, written by Blaikie for the purse of $6,000, which was deposited in Blaikie's name in a bank in Rochester, but when Hanlan took the check to the bank a few days later, the cashier said Hanlan could not have the money because the certificate of deposit, which Soule had, had to accompany the check and be signed by Soule. Soule refused to give up the certificate of deposit on the grounds that the conditions of the race and the prize demanded that both men row.

Soule offered an award of $1,000 for the apprehension of the person who sawed the boats. Brister added $500 to that. Later some of the New York newspapers hired detectives to try to solve the mystery.

The little community of Mayville had never seen such "sharpies" before. "Every swindle known to dishonesty was practiced with impunity at Mayville," the Jamestown reporter wrote. The *Syracuse Courier* said, "The developments of today created a feeling of widespread disgust, the result of which will be to discourage public attention in future sporting events. . . ." Other papers echoed this feeling, saying that the real victims were the spectators who had no way of knowing whether a competition was honest or not, but now would probably consider all contests crooked. They predicted a quick demise for many spectator sports.

In Canada, the papers said that never again could the enthusiasm be aroused which greeted Hanlan during his former contests. The conduct of his backers at Chautauqua "throws a doubt around him. The sport in the Dominion has received its death blow."

The editor of the *Troy Times,* Charles S. Francis who was a skilled sculler and Cornellian, said:

> It seems as if never since the firing on Fort Sumter did an event so arouse the anger of the American people. In every city, village and hamlet, wherever a telegraph wire or a newspaper penetrated, the storm of indignation raged. And, not strange at all to relate, but perfectly natural, as has always been the case from time immemorial, the majority did not place the blame where it belongs, but in their blind and unreasonable anger, accused Courtney of sawing his own boat, the last man on earth who would have done such a thing. His whole racing career . . . had been without a suspicion and without reproach. He never touched a drop of liquor, he did not use tobacco, he did not gamble, he knew no fast companions. . . .

What happened? Hanlan, whose convivial habits were well known, had been out the day before. He had listened to the voice of the charmer and apparently had forgotten all about the race. His friends and backers became alarmed. A conference was held with Courtney that same night, and efforts were made to postpone the race. When these failed, the entire purse of $6,000 was offered him if he would consent to make the race a draw. The reply was characteristic of the man [Courtney]. 'Gentlemen,' he said, 'the race will be rowed tomorrow, and whoever wins it will have to row for it!' A suspicion of foul play never entered his head.

A few days after the aborted race, Soule made a new offer to Courtney, saying that if Courtney would row five miles on any course within three months, under the usual rules, and beat Hanlan's time, Hop Bitters would give him a purse of $1,000. Courtney and his friends and backers met at his home to discuss the offer. Courtney said, as quoted in the *Auburn Daily Advertiser*:

I'd like to row just to satisfy the public, but it would cost me a good deal. I would have to pay $125 for a new boat right off, and then it is getting late and I might have to wait some time before I could have a good day—and if I row I shall wait 'til I have just as good water as Hanlan had. Besides, I should have to run the risk of catching cold. I have lost already $1,200 or $1,300 and I don't feel like spending any more unless I can make something.

Now if Mr. Soule would offer me $2,000 or $3,000, or $100 for every second by which I beat Hanlan's time, I would jump at the chance. If I accept Mr. Soule's offer, I shall probably row on Owasco Lake. The surveyor will make an affidavit that it is a full five miles.

The Auburn paper commented that in his conversation about Hanlan and his party, Courtney used no harsh names and said no mean words. "When the public has had time to consider the facts in the case, its sympathy will be with the Union Springs oarsman, and we defy any fair-minded man to converse with him (Courtney) without being convinced that he is innocent of any attempt to avoid a race with Hanlan," the account continued.

Courtney seemed to think favorably of Soule's offer, the paper said, as he desires to show by his time that he could beat Hanlan, while his backers oppose his making the best time possible for him, because it would preclude the possibility of making any bets afterward.

The offer was turned down, but still Soule said he would back Courtney in any future race for any amount.

Within the next few weeks, Courtney signed affidavits in Rochester attesting to several conversations in which Hanlan's men had tried to buy him off, either for part or for all of the purse. One of these conversations had been heard by Frenchy while eavesdropping outside Courtney's boathouse.

Talks about another race continued for several weeks, with Chautauqua Lake, Rochester, and Washington, D.C. mentioned as possible sites. There were reports that Courtney had accepted Soule's offer to beat Hanlan's time, but he did not accept the offer. Then there was word that the two men were to row on Chautauqua Lake in early November, and if it was too cold, they were to row at Washington, D.C.

Finally, after many plans for a race were made and then cancelled, the two men were to row on December 9 at Rochester for a purse of $6,000 put up by Soule. Courtney took sick with nephritis and lumbago and was confined to his home in Union Springs, so this race was never held. Courtney stayed in Union Springs, recuperating from his illness. His backers said he could not row until spring. Hanlan went to England where he rowed in other competitions.

After several months of negotiations, a date was set for an encounter at Washington, D.C. on the Potomac River on May 19, 1880. The rules were the same as for the Chautauqua Lake race. Again the purse was $6,000, offered by Soule. Again Blaikie was the referee.

The day before the race, again the gamblers were everywhere, following the crowds who filled the Capital. Reserved seats on riverboats were in great demand. Throngs claimed places along the shoreline long before the race. The betting was 100 to 80 in favor of Hanlan.

Courtney had rowed eight miles on the river for a practice run, and had complained of a severe headache the day before the race. His trainers said he was acutely affected by the heat, but he was prepared to start at the scheduled time, late in the afternoon.

Hanlan won the toss for the choice of the lane, and, on the advice of his trainers, took the Virginia side.

On the day of the race, even the oppressive heat did not deter the crowds. President Rutherford B. Hayes and some of his cabinet members were on the referee's launch. U.S. Navy boats and armed police patrolled the course.

As the two men rowed leisurely to the starting line from their boathouses, the crowds cheered. At the word, "Go," the two slim boats shot forward. At first Courtney's oar seemed to catch a trifle ahead of Hanlan's, and with a steady, even grip upon the water, he sent his boat ahead. For the first few minutes he pulled at the rate of 36 strokes a minute, while Hanlan did 41, the Jamestown reporter wrote in his account. Hanlan soon took the lead and with each succeeding stroke, he went farther to the fore. At the first flag marking an eighth of a mile from the start, clear water could be seen between the stern of Hanlan's boat and the bow of Courtney's.

At this point, Courtney turned to look over his shoulder and suddenly dropped his stroke to 30 strokes a minute and shook his head. Someone on the referee's boat shouted to him to pull. Courtney called, "It isn't in me."

Hanlan eased to 32 strokes when he reached the three-quarter mile flag, fully ten lengths ahead. At the first mile he was pulling 31 strokes to the minute, leading Courtney by fully fifteen boat lengths.

Courtney, laboring unsteadily at about 28 strokes, frequently cast a despairing glance over his shoulder. He soon removed his handkerchief, dipped it in the water and replaced it on his head. He repeated this half a dozen times during the next mile. His steering, which at the start was faultless, became more and more erratic. Three of the six flags from the half-mile to the two-mile point were either brushed by his oars or run over directly by his boat, according to the Jamestown paper.

Courtney stopped finally, three-eighths of a mile from the turn, and two and an eighth of a mile from the start. He turned his boat and pulled leisurely back over the course and disembarked at his quarters at the Potomac boathouse.

When Courtney was returning to the boathouse, both men were going in the same direction. Hanlan had made the turn, but Courtney was out of the race. This confused thousands of spectators on the shore and in the boats along the river. Not knowing that Courtney had not gone around the buoy marking the turn, they imagined the race was still underway and they "rent the air with cheers."

Hanlan soon passed Courtney and leisurely pulled to the last eighth of a mile and then quickened his speed to 40 strokes, exhibiting a splendid burst of speed at the finish.

After passing the finish line, Hanlan worked his way through the boats to the dock where he was lifted bodily from his boat by his friends and was carried on their shoulders. He was congratulated by Blaikie and Soule. This time he received the $6,000. Later he was serenaded at his hotel in Washington. His comment to reporters was that he "came to row a race and very much regretted that he had not been able to do so."

There was another oarsman rowing just outside the race course who distracted many of the viewers. He was James Riley, who had rowed a dead heat with Hanlan the year before. He had tried to get in this race but was turned down because this was to be strictly a Courtney-Hanlan contest. Riley was prepared to enter the race if either Hanlan or Courtney failed to appear. Since both of them were there, Riley started rowing outside the course, beginning just a few seconds before the signal was given to start. He continued along the direction of the course about an eighth of a mile ahead of Hanlan, so that some people thought he was winning a great victory.

Courtney's trainers said they had urged him not to enter the race because they knew he was weakened by the heat, but he had insisted on rowing. They said he was particularly sensitive to the heat and was severely affected by it because he had had a sunstroke several years before. They had frowned on his eight-mile practice rowing session the day before. They said he had not slept the night before the race and had eaten very little for several days.

This race seemed to close the Courtney-Hanlan controversy that had started as the "race of the century" and ended as "the

Chautauqua Lake Fizzle," as some of the papers billed it if they did not label it "The Fiasco." It also cast suspicion on the operators who promoted the races, leaving the public with feelings of disgust and undoubtedly leading to the decline of interest in professional rowing as a sport.

From Courtney and Cornell Rowing

Courtney in racing trim in 1879

CHAPTER 9

THE AFTERMATH

The bloom was off professional sculling after the Chautauqua Lake race and the subsequent encounter between Courtney and Hanlan on the Potomac River in May 1880. A disgusted public gave sculling races less and less attention. But stories of that era prevailed for many years, and even today make "good copy," as newsmen say.

One such tale comes from Chautauqua County, the scene of the aborted race and the infamous dealings of the gamblers. The following account was sent to the author by Robert G. Wright, an attorney in Jamestown, New York.

> Not only did the regatta attract the boating and betting fraternity, but it also drew a periphery of petty thieves and pickpockets who plied their nefarious trade among the gala crowds. The late Marion H. Fisher, prominent Jamestown attorney, delighted in telling this story about his father, Chautauqua County Judge Jerome B. Fisher.
>
> As Judge Fisher strolled about Mayville on the day before the scheduled race, enjoying the holiday atmosphere and greeting friends, he suddenly became aware that his gold watch and chain were missing. He sought out the sheriff, who suggested that they meet at a certain hotel in an hour.
>
> When Judge Fisher arrived, there was a message for him to come to one of the rooms. A knock at the door brought admittance. There stood the sheriff with two of the shady characters and there, on the bed, more than 50 watches were laid out. Judge Fisher quickly spotted his timepiece and returned it to his vest pocket. As he was leaving the room, he overheard the sheriff admonishing the culprits to be more careful in selecting future victims.

Even though many decades have passed since the Chautauqua Lake Fizzle, the controversy has not ended. Some students from Courtney's hometown found a letter to him among some rowing memorabilia at Cornell University. It was dated July 16, 1900—almost twenty-one years after the aborted race—from A. Wilson Dods of Fredonia, New York saying that he got a statement from Ed Irwin Jr. of Chautauqua, whose father, Ed Irwin Sr., heard Courtney's boats being sawed. The elder Irwin owned the boathouse next to Courtney's.

On May 8, 1900, the younger Irwin gave Dods an account of what happened at Courtney's boathouse, saying that a day or two before the race he had seen Hanlan and his backers come to see Courtney at his boathouse, heard them offer to buy off Courtney, who replied that he would not do it. Then the Hanlan crowd left.

The evening before the race, Irwin Sr. said Courtney's backer let Courtney's brother and another man go to Mayville to get shaved, saying he would look after the boats. About dusk Irwin Sr. saw the backer coming to the boathouse with a saw, heard the sound of sawing and then saw the man throw the saw in the lake, the statement said.

Dods, who took the statement from the younger Irwin, said that the only explanation he had for the concealment of these facts was that the elder Irwin let Courtney's backer know he was caught and was bought off to keep his mouth shut and that his son Ed Irwin would not speak during his father's lifetime.

The complete statement was:

66 East Main Street
Fredonia, New York

Statement made to me by Ed Irwin of Chautauqua, New York on the afternoon of May 8th, 1900.

I called on Mr. Irwin on the afternoon of May 8th and during the conversation happened to mention that I had been at Ithaca and seen Chas. Courtney. This led to the statement that he [Irwin] knew Mr. Courtney well when he was on Chautuauqua Lake in 1879; that their boathouses were side by side and to the inquiry if I knew who it was who sawed Mr. Courtney's boats, he then told the following.

A day or two before the race, Hanlan, his backer and I think he said one or two others, came and interviewed Mr. Courtney in his boathouse, Mr. Courtney being alone at the time. They did not know that he [Irwin] was in his boathouse alongside and in a few minutes the voices were so loud that they could have been heard at a much greater distance than Irwin's boathouse. The matter under discussion was the buying off of Mr. Courtney and the root of the subject was reached by Mr. Courtney declaring "That he knew he could beat Hanlan, that Hanlan also knew it, that all his [Courtney's] friends had their money on him and that he was not going to sell them out, that if Hanlan won that race he would have to do it square by so far as he [Courtney] was concerned." This ended the matter and the Hanlan crowd left.

The evening before the race Courtney's backer (I have forgotten the name) allowed Mr. Courtney's brother and the other man to go to Mayville for the purpose of getting shaved prior to race day, he agreeing to look after the boats too during their absence.

About dusk Mr. Ed Irwin's father was in their boathouse and saw Courtney's backer come to Courtney's boathouse carrying something under his coat, he had to take it out and set it down so as to open the boathouse door, when (the) elder Irwin saw it was a saw. The backer went into the boathouse and immediately the sound of sawing was heard, in a few minutes the backer came out on the dock or float and threw the saw as far out into the lake as he could. When Mr. Courtney's brother and the man came back, the boat or boats were found sawed in two.

This is Irwin's statement. The only explanation I can offer for the concealment of these facts is that the elder Irwin let Courtney's backer know that he was caught and was bought off to keep his mouth shut, and that his son Ed Irwin for his father's sake would not speak during his father's lifetime."

The letter Dods wrote to Courtney with the statement was:

Chautauqua, N.Y. July 15, 1900
Mr. Chas. Courtney
Ithaca, N. Y.

Dear Sir:

I sincerely hope you will take the enclosed communication in the spirit in which I send it to you, viz that were I in your place and you in mine, I feel that I should wish to know the facts stated even if it were an opening to some extent of old wounds. So please consider that it is in the *kindliest* spirit that I act and believe me to be,

Yours very truly,
(signed)
A. Wilson Dods

Until August 20, 1900 [I will be at]
Box 468
Chautauqua, New York

Courtney's reaction to the statement is unknown. There is no record of any comment in his papers at the Cornell University Archives. Courtney's character and integrity were not questioned by those who knew him well at the time of the Chautauqua Lake episode, nor by any who knew him afterward. At the time and down through the years, the general opinion has been that Courtney himself was not involved in the damaging of his boats. In 1879 Courtney was a relatively unsophisticated young man, an athletic celebrity who was used by others. Whether the culprits came from his camp or from Hanlan's camp or from some other group remains a mystery.

In his book, *Courtney And Cornell Rowing,* C. V. P. Young says: "Whenever in the course of his long and busy life the matter was broached with some heat now and again by one of his friends, he always waved him aside with, 'Never mind, my boy; it will all come out right in the end.' "

Hanlan continued to row professionally in America, England and Australia until 1897. Also, he continued to be popular with Canadians, who covered him with flattery. He was the world rowing champion from 1880 to 1884 when he lost the title to William Beach, an Australian. He was Canada's first international sports hero. For a few years he coached rowing at the University of Toronto and at Columbia University. When he died in 1908 he was given a state funeral.

Courtney also continued to row in races as a professional for a few years and at exhibitions. He continued to operate the New York Planing Mill and Hub Works with his brother John and coached the women's seminary and college crews, the local club crews and individuals in his free time. He was part owner of a sailing yacht and took part in some of the races on Cayuga Lake.

There is evidence that on one occasion he later encountered Hanlan in a race. It is recorded in a letter to his wife Della from Toronto on September 4, 1881. Besides mentioning a race with Hanlan, the letter shows Courtney's succinct observations and self-confidence. It reads:

Toronto
Septmber 4, 1881

Dear Della,

I have not had time to write you before tonight. We did not get here the day we started until 11:30, and a dirtier set (of people) you never saw. The whole country around here is on fire. The city is so full of smoke, we can hardly breath. It is better tonight than it has been any day since we have been here. We are having a good time here. The people are very kind to us and the papers treat us very fair, but they think I can't row.

I had a race with Hanlan yesterday and got the best of him and think I will beat him in the race. (Wallace) Ross is rowing very fast and has a better boat than I have, but at the same time, if they give me a fair show I will make him row faster than he ever went in his life if he wins the money. The betting here beats anything I ever saw.

I will try and write you before the race if I can get time. Remember me to all the folks.

Ever yours,
Charlie.

For some unknown reason, Hanlan did not enter the race Courtney mentioned. Courtney came in third after Ross who was first and Conley, second.

Courtney and Hanlan probably had some contacts when Hanlan coached the Columbia University crew from 1900 to 1903, while Courtney was training the Cornell crews, who were piling up victories.

The above letter of September 4 to his wife seems to be one of a several he wrote to her in the fall of 1881 when he was making a circuit and competing in three or four races. It was customary for oarsmen to enter several contests within a few weeks during the good rowing season. Again on Septmber 14 he wrote:

(no place given)
September 14, 1881

Dear Della,

Today has been a big day in Fulton (New York). I never saw as many people at a county fair, and I never saw so much dust. We have our boats in the Baptist Society's refreshment house. They are very nice people and take great deal of pride in pointing out Riley and myself to the crowd.

They had a balloon ascension here today and it was the finest one I ever saw. A young woman by the name of Thurston went in the balloon. I would rather go a-foot.

Friday, if it is pleasant, will be a great day here. There is nothing talked of here but the boat race and Courtney. James Vick of Rochester has a floral exhibit on the grounds. It is the finest thing I ever saw. It is simply immense. There were 8,000 people on the grounds, and it is safe to say 5,000 were women. There are a great many folks here from Auburn, Weedsport and Syracuse. They are to run special trains on all the Roads Friday. They think they will have 20,000 people here Friday, and judging from what I have seen, I think they will.

The crowd has commenced to gather around the hotel and the only show for me is to get out. It is fearful to have a dozen talking in my ears all at once. Remember me to all the folks. Will telegraph if I conclude to come on Saturday.

Charlie.

Another letter from Rochester, New York, was written on September 27. He wrote after a race on the Genesee River:

Rochester, N.Y.
September 27, 1881

Dear Della,

We leave here in the morning at 7:15 for Cazenovia (New York). If nothing happens, I will be in U.S. (Union Springs) on Saturday.We are going to row at Elmira about the 12th of October. We had quite a race today. Lee beat Riley and James (Riley) doesn't feel very well over it. Plaisted quit at the stake boat. I didn't have to row very hard to win.

It is nearly twelve o'clock. Guess I will retire. You can look for me home Saturday.

Charlie.

When talking to Professor Hewett about his racing career, Courtney said,

The hardest race I ever rowed was the double-scull race at Saratoga with Frank Yates as partner. That was the fastest race for two miles ever rowed in this or any other country, in that kind of boat. The record, 12:16 stands today (1905). I rowed at Aurora, in a single scull, against a double scull, two miles in 13:10, but it was never allowed, owing to that technicality. The fastest mile I ever made—

> timed by myself, by my own watch, so that I know it was absolutley correct—was in 6 minutes. My best record in a race for a mile and a half is 9:46, although I have rowed it exactly in 9 minutes in practice.

At the end of his professional rowing career, Courtney had rowed 46 races and lost 7. It was not such a perfect record as his amateur score—88 races rowed and not a one lost—but he was still considered a champion oarsmen, one of the greatest of all time. In the estimation of many people he was just as good as Hanlan, if not better. Others thought they were a close match. The Canadians, of course, said their "Neddie" was the best sculler of all time.

Courtney was still a young man when he gave up rowing professionally. Like some of the other professionals, he became the coach of a college crew. His college and crew were down Cayuga Lake at Ithaca, where he had become acquainted with the Cornell Navy, as the oarsmen were called.

At first the colleges did not want to be associated with the professional oarsmen and their questionable backers. But from the early 1880s on, the names of professional scullers appear on the rosters of coaches. Mendenhall, in *A Short History of American Rowing,* says it was inevitable that the professional scullers would creep back into the picture as coaches and bring with them "some of their tricks and more secretiveness about their crews and their progress than was good for the sport. Yet their knowledge and experience was invaluable." He describes Courtney as perhaps the most famous and successful of the professional oarsmen who became coaches.

Courtney began his association with Cornell rowing in 1883 when he coached the crew for about ten days. With the exception of the next year, 1884, when John Teemer was in charge of the crew, Courtney was asscoiated with the Cornell crews until his death in 1920.

CHAPTER 10

A NEW CAREER—COACHING

When Courtney was hired by Cornell University for ten days in 1883 to coach the varsity crew, he probably did not realize that he was starting on a new career in which he would distinguish himself as much, if not more, than he had as a champion sculler. He had been coaching the women at the Seminary and at Howland College in Union Springs, the village's boating club crew and a number of young men who aspired to being champion scullers. So coaching was not new to him, but it was his avocation. He was still rowing occasionally in exhibitions and races and operating the Central New York Planing Mill with his brother John.

To his coaching tasks he brought more than his knowledge of rowing and how to rig boats, more than his carpentry skills that he often used in repairing and even building boats. He brought a natural ability to inspire and gain the confidence of his students. Although throughout the years he was very strict, he was very fair and thus gained the respect and devotion of the crews he trained.

Courtney started coaching at Cornell when its policies regarding athletics were in their infancy. His own attitudes and policies, therefore, greatly influenced the standards that were set. He insisted that the men who rowed under him must keep up their university work first. Therefore, to the faculty he was not a rival but a fellow educator.

In the Cornell University Archives there are several sheets of notes, written by Courtney, that appear to be reminders of significant events in the past. They might have been written in anticipation of a speech he was going to give. The first notations indicate that he had an interest in the university long before he arrived to coach a crew there. These intriguing notes make us wish we knew the stories and events he had in mind. The heading is "CHARLES COURTNEY NOTES." The first five notations, separated by a line across the page are:

> The first Cornell Boathouse built by the Boys. Story of how I thought President Adams was the sheriff [who had] come to collect 15 dollars for rent of land.
>
> * * *
>
> Race between Cornell and Union Springs crew. Story about sliding seats; how they stuck and how the *Cornell Sun* thought it too bad that lot of country boys should have modern things and Cornell not.
>
> * * *
>
> 1873 Crew. Cornell's first varsity six-oared crew. Story of Philips putting up window curtains for Millie Peterson, and building the four-oared shell for Union Springs crew in which they won the Watkins regatta.
>
> * * *
>
> 1876 Crew—one of the finest rowing crews Cornell ever turned out, bar none.
>
> * * *
>
> 1878 Freshman crew rowed on Owasco Lake and beat Harvard. How [it] came to change training quarters and how easily they beat . . . afterward."

The next entry skips a decade and refers to an 1888 crew, which was under his tutelage and is a later story, as are the other entries.

In 1883 he was asked to take over the training of a badly equipped and almost untrained crew. The *Cornell Era* said three of the men were utterly inexperienced in racing, and the fourth had rowed in one losing race. This four-oared boat, under constant and careful training under the "able instruction of Courtney" mastered the "git thar" stroke and won the race on Lake George by 32 seconds, beating Pennsylvania and Princeton, who had been considered the leading crews that year, as well as Columbia and Wesleyan.

This crew used roller-made seats, an idea conceived and

Cornell Archives

The first Cornell boathouse, built by the students.

worked out by Courtney in his own racing. In his early racing days, he had used the old, sliding seat. He replaced this with a seat on rollers, arranged so that the axles on which the wheels revolve were not held in one place but moved back and forth with a motion that gave the occupants of the boat the greatest ease and freedom in their movements. At first he used big, wooden rollers, but found that the position of the men in the shallow boat required smaller rollers to bring the center of gravity as low as possible.

At this time, intercollegiate athletic competitions involving Cornell were few, probably because the University was reluctant to grant permission for out-of-town trips. Some of the universities objected to the professionalism that threatened college athletics and the vices, such as pool selling, bookmaking and disorderly conduct, that accompanied it nearer large cities. In 1884 Cornell joined with eleven other colleges to condemn professional coaching and the holding of contests away from college campuses. But this was voted down by the Intercollegiate Athletic Association. During the 1884 season John

Teemer coached the Cornell crews because Courtney was busy with his work and some professional rowing.

It is generally agreed that Courtney became the regular coach of Cornell's crews in 1885. After that he rowed very few races. In spite of some disagreements over contracts and what he considered the needs of the crews throughout the years, he continued his active coaching career there until 1916 when he became part-time coach because he had not completely recovered from a bad bump on his head received on a train going to Poughkeepsie in 1915. He, however, was on hand often for practice sessions, giving advice when it was needed until his death in 1920.

Some people have said that an agreement in the Cornell University Archives, dated April 20, 1888 between Courtney and the Athletic Council covering his salary, signifies that he started as the regular coach in 1888, but three Cornell historians, C. V. P. Young, Morris Bishop and Professor Waterman Thomas Hewett, agree that he was at the university for a short time in 1883 and returned as regular coach in 1885. Courtney's niece, Nellie Larmon Anthony, agrees with them in her biography, *The Master Coach.*

The year 1885 marks the beginning of Cornell's "monotonous record of supremacy," as Morris Bishop described the many victories of the crews. During Courtney's coaching period he trained approximately 146 intercollegiate crews, which were victorious in 101 races. These included 14 victories out of 24 Intercollegiate Rowing Association varsity contests. This reputation for victories in a popular college sport helped the public's general recognition of the young university.

Courtney had been in touch with the developing university on the hill above Ithaca ever since the first buildings were erected. Besides competing against some of its scullers in the early 1870s when John Ostrom was in charge of the crews, Courtney had visited the campus on several occasions. On one of his early visits to the "Godless Institution," as the papers called it, he had noted that timbers and building materials were lying about, mud was ankle deep, and walkways were erratic.

But on later trips to Ithaca, he had seen order develop out of this seeming chaos, he had noticed that the students were plucky and rugged, and he had seen some of the early baseball games on a field belonging to Ezra Cornell.

Courtney quickly showed himself to be a master of men. Those who went out for rowing soon learned that he set the same high standards for them that he had set for himself. These involved habits of self-discipline, healthy eating and living, honesty and devotion to the task at hand. He was strict; but he was fair. In spite of a seeming harshness of manner and imperturbability, his "boys" loved him. He was a quiet person, and with an unassuming demeanor. He was seldom seen in public except on business matters or in connection with his work.

During the first few years that he coached the crews, there was always the question of whether or not there would be enough money for the University's Navy. The other sports were barely self-supporting; rowing was in no way a money-maker. It was supported by the Athletic Association which got voluntary subscriptions from the alumni and undergraduates, and seldom had sufficient funds for the crews. Every October a day was appointed "upon which we should all join in bringing our offerings to the treasury of the Cornell Navy for the specific purpose of meeting the annual salary of our Navy coach," said Professor Benjamin Ide Wheeler, the faculty's liaison with the rowing program. This meant that Courtney's salary and the money he needed for equipment were seldom sure things he could count on from one year to the next. And, although he was employed by the Athletic Association and had no official connection with the University, he still functioned as a colleague of the others who taught, for he regarded himself as a teacher of rowing.

In the 1888 agreement in the Cornell University Archives, the Athletic Council agreed to pay him $15 a week during the rowing season, with $10 to be paid weekly and the remaining $5 withheld until said services were fully performed. The council also agreed to pay Courtney's board and travelling expenses as long as he was with the crew.

Cornell Archives

Courtney talking with crew candidates in the 1890s.

This was the same year that the rowing program was in one of its usual financial squeezes. A new shell was needed, but there weren't any funds. A total of $123 was owed to Courtney. So, a rally was held to raise funds, this being a common practice in those days. After the debt to Courtney was cleared up, he was introduced with the following high praise: "The famous and highly successful coach, Charles E. Courtney, has agreed to coach again this year. His judgment and skill are well known."

Courtney responded with words that expressed the philosophy and tenets of coaching that he used throughout his career:

> No man should come out for the crew who is not ready to give the best he has. If he expects to succeed, he must be an enthusiastic, a hard and faithful worker, a conscientious trainer, and a man who feels at all times that the honor and glory of his university are

> entrusted to his care. Only those men can be selected in whom not only the captain and the coach, but every man in the boat, has full confidence. A particular man may not always be the most skillful individual oarsman, but he is part of a machine and the fact that eight men must be chosen who will work as one man must always be kept in mind. How can a crew row a hard race when there is one man in the boat whose sand will give out when the final test comes? Furthermore, the training a man undergoes as a member of the University crew sends him out into the world not only with a sound, healthy body, but also with the habits of regularity, promptness, obedience, and self-control thoroughly ground into him, and I have never found a crew man who regarded the time and labor as ill-spent. In almost every case, he looks back upon the experience as one of the most pleasant as well as most profitable of his college courses.

The uncertainty of being able to get equipment, due to financial difficulties, meant that Courtney used his skills as a boatbuilder to make many repairs and adjustments. He was at the boathouse early in the morning, even when the crews were not expected to row, working on the shells, oars, outriggers, putting a new deck on a boat or patching an older one.

Courtney's reputation as a coach soon spread, bringing him offers from other colleges to come and coach their crews. These probably were tempting, in view of the annual hassle to raise funds at Cornell. The newspaper would hear of offers he had received and then would run, as with a sigh of relief, such

Cornell Archives

Courtney standing on the shore, watching the 1892 crew practice.

statements as, "We are happy to chronicle the fact that Courtney is to stay. Early in the week he refused to consider several flattering offers from other places and decided to remain. Courtney is going to stay!"

Courtney finally had enough of the uncertainties. He asked that a guarantee fund be raised to assure him a more definite proof that his services were wanted than he had received in the past. He had several tempting offers to go elsewhere, which spurred the student newspaper to call for support of the fund. A petition was put in the library, and every man and woman in the University was urged to sign "as a small token of the anxiety which is felt at the startling possibilities that Cornell's crews should be without the rigid and thorough training which only Courtney can give them . . . Courtney and Cornell are inseparable." The immediate, enthusiastic response from the students pleased Courtney so much that he promised to remain at Cornell, even before the fund was assured.

He had stipulated that an agreement be reached by October 11, 1894, and it was. An agreement, signed by Courtney and Professor Wheeler for the Athletic Association, remains today in the Archives. It stipulates that Courtney will get $1200 for his services the first year; $1350 the second year; and $1500, the third year. And he will have two weeks of vacation in August.

The promise and agreement did not keep him from accepting an invitation for a two-week visit from Harvard, which had been trying to get him to coach there. The Harvard staff reported afterward that they derived great benefits from Courtney's visit, learning much about blade work and rigging the boat. When Courtney returned to Ithaca, he was greeted by enthusiastic crowds of students. He thanked them for their greetings, then said, "I have been away on a vacation, but now I hope to get back to work. There will probably be no call for crew condidates before January 1, and when the call does come, it will be of no use for any to offer himself unless he is well up with his University work."

When the call did come for crew candidates, 153 men reported for work on the rowing machines in the gymnasium.

Probably two thirds of these men were really trying for the crew; the rest were there for the exercise and to learn a little about the stroke. They had heard Courtney say that he felt there is no better exercise than rowing. He broadcast the fact that the rowing machines were available to anyone who wanted to use them at any time except between five and six in the afternoon when the machines were reserved for the crew. He was in the crew room from one to six every day.

By the crews he meant the varsity, junior varsity and freshmen. Besides these eight-oared boats, there were four-oared boats. The six-oared boats were used for the last time in intercollegiate competition involving Cornell in 1876.

How did he pick the men for the crews? "I have to pick my preliminary material before I see the boys on the water," Courtney told Professor Hewett. He continued:

> To do this, I watch the men in the gymnasium, and ascertain their disposition and temperament. To be a desirable man for crew, a student must not only have a good physique, but he must be willing, have a high moral character, and be an excellent student. I will not take any man who is not of good moral character, nor will I take one who is not doing well in his university work. I have found by experience that the best students make the best oarsmen. . . . If I find a man getting behind in his university work, I drop him at once.

Courtney's keen observation is apparent in his further statements about how he selected the crews:

> It is the systematic men who are of the most service in a boat, as everywhere else. There are some students who are without a balance wheel. They will come rushing into the boathouse and throw their coats one way and their hats another. For these men I have no patience. The man who comes to the boathouse the exact minute he has promised to be there, who hangs up his clothes methodically, dons his rowing costume and goes out in the boat quietly, and without any "hurrah" about it, is pretty sure to be the man who will do the hardest work in a race, and who can be depended upon not to go to pieces in a pinch. If you get one disturbing element in a boat, one man who is a growler or grumbler, you will always have trouble to make that crew row fast.

Courtney also had a device he invented that helped him

select the men for his crews. It was a machine for measuring the new recruits. Hewett explains it this way:

> They [the men] are placed in position and every racing quality is accurately gauged, so that the trainer knows just what part of the boat they will fit to the best advantage, keeping in mind the other material already in the crew. There is one peculiarity about the operation on this machine, and that is that while the students have seen hundreds measured on this machine they have never yet seen their trainer take down a figure, and yet after the operation is over he knows the man he has measured so accurately and has his proportions so strongly impressed on his mind, that he can at any time thereafter place him according to the measurement.

By April, when the crews could get on the water, Courtney said the candidates were usually sifted down to sixteen. He lamented that Cornell (in Courtney's time) did not have rowing tanks, as did Yale and Harvard. But he felt the Cornellians who wanted to row had an advantage in their training in being compelled to climb the steep Ithaca hills each day, going to and from the University. This exercise, he felt, develops the muscles of their legs, and for that reason the Courtney style of rowing, which demands a great deal of work from the legs, is particularly well-adapted to the Cornell crews.

Courtney's strict adherence to his principle of honesty was deeply impressed on one group of Cornell oarsmen. In the boathouse one afternoon, Courtney overheard a crew member telling another how he had passed an examination by irregular means. Quick as a flash, Courtney turned around and pointed to the door, saying. "Young man, go right upstairs, put on your clothes, and get out of this boathouse. A man who will cheat in an examination will quit in a boat race, and I never want to see you down here again."

There were other days when his crews saw the side of Courtney that still loved to row, that enjoyed their company. Often, in his early years of coaching the Cornell crews, he would launch his single scull, give the crew a practice in starts, and row a distance with them down the lake.

Whether he was watching them from his single scull or from the railroad embankment along the shore, his eagle eye missed nothing. When he saw something that needed attention, he blew a whistle to signal the crew to stop. Then he hurried down the bank and shouted instructions. In later years he had a launch in which he followed the crews.

Courtney's philosophy that rowing was good exercise for everyone led to the expansion of his program to include intramural competition for both men and women. The Women's Boating Club was formed in 1897. They were given machine practice at Courtney's home in the winter, and when the weather permitted in the spring they rowed on the Inlet of Cayuga Lake several times a week at six o'clock in the morning. In the early 1900s they rowed on Beebe Lake on the campus.

Courtney also fostered intramural racing, between the University's colleges. This meant that by the early 1900s there was not room enough in the regular boathouse to accomodate these intramural oarsmen. They were not the caliber for the varsity competition yet were sufficiently adept to compete in minor races, and Courtney urged that they have opportunities to row. Under his supervision and with the support of the Physical Education Department, a separate boathouse was built. Several of the colleges supplied the boats. About 200

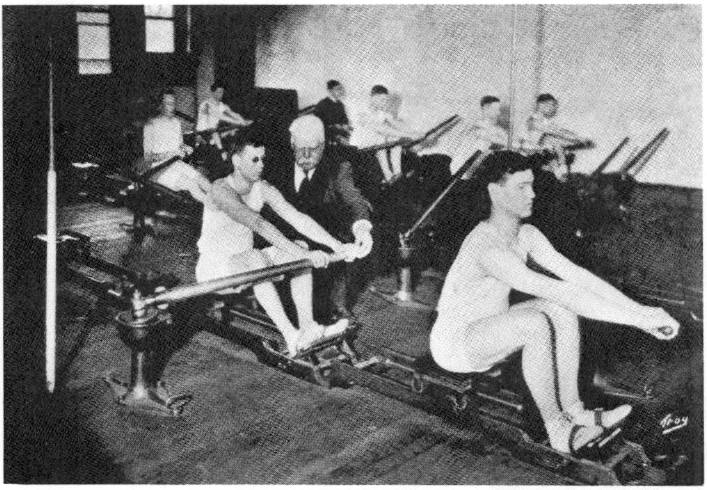

From Courtney and Cornell Rowing

Courtney encouraged blind students to use rowing machines.

men trained for these crews, and regular races were established. These crews often proved to be the training ground and the source of men for the varsities.

Blind students were encouraged by Courtney to use the rowing machines. Young, Courtney's biographer who knew him well, says:

> A vivid picture still remains in the mind of the writer of Mr. Courtney patiently instructing two blind students in the intricacies of the stroke, and the pleasure with which he watched their progress and their ability to perfectly time their stroke in unison with the other oarsmen.

Courtney's notes, which he may have made as reminders of incidents to include in a speech, and which are in the Archives, as mentioned above, continue with notations from the following years:

> 1888. Four won two races at Philadelphia. Were to have rowed in the National at Sunbury. Why they didn't. Story of going out with the girls.

* * *

> 1889. The first Cornell varsity eight. Story of Joe Colmon going down the lake with girl. Story of my old boss, Mr. Jaquith, from whom I learned my trade. How he saw the race at Philadelphia. How I fooled the boys by not putting any grease on the oars and beat them.

* * *

> 1890. Crew story of Upton putting dole back on the seat after he jumped off from it. Story Upton acting the part of a crazy man on our way back from New London.

* * *

> 1891. This crew holds the record for 3 miles. How the boats got mixed. Penn got ours and we got theirs.

* * *

> 1892. This crew won on the Passaic and on Cayuga Lake. Story of putting shellac on seats. How I took a row down to Estys and back with this crew. Story of how Troy came out for crew and how his father saw him row in a relay race on the lake.

* * *

1893. Rowed at Minnetonka. Freshmen rowed at New London. How I followed the varsity west after the Freshman race. My reception by the boys. They were not a bit glad to see me. They were having a good time with the girls. What I told the mother of one of the girls and the judge.

* * *

1894. At Torrace Dale. Story of Chick Freeborn catching a crab and getting knocked overboard.

* * *

1895. Henley crew. Story of my horseback ride.

We wish we knew all these stories, many of which must have made Courtney laugh as he made note of them. The last notation, the Henley crew, was the first American eight-oared boat to go to the races at Henley, England.

Cornell Archives

Charles Courtney in the early 1890s.

CHAPTER 11

THE CREW GOES TO HENLEY

The year 1895 will be remembered as the year Cornell sent the first American eight-oared boat to the prestigious Henley Regatta on the Thames River in England to compete for the Grand Challenge Cup. The experience was long remembered and discussed on the Cornell campus, partly because of its unfortunate results, but also because it brought the American college oarsmen in contact with their British counterparts, thus arousing many comparisons of the different strokes, customs and training methods.

By 1895 the Cornell crews were accustomed to Courtney's strict discipline, his almost autocratic rule over them and his vigilant care of them and their equipment. All these traits were apparent during the Henley experience.

The training rules and diet that Courtney established for his crews were much more sensible than the practices used in the early days of rowing when trainees were expected to walk or row long distances before breakfast. In the early days, the men were allowed nothing but raw beef or mutton, potatoes, bread, tea and water. Potatoes were served sparingly, and trainees were not allowed to eat any other vegetable. Tea was given them only on special occasions, and water was in some instances limited to one glass for breakfast, two for dinner and one for supper. There was also a custom of bundling up and working until drenched in perspiration in order to reduce weight.

By Courtney's coaching days things had changed, and he himself was a strong advocate of sensible eating and exercising habits. He found that with strenuous physical exercise, an oarsman's appetite was so sharpened that he craved only solid and nourishing foods, and if he had plenty of these he was perfectly satisfied without the less nourishing dishes and those more difficult to digest. Courtney recommended a liberal supply of beef, mutton or fowl, vegetables of all kinds, as many eggs as man wanted to eat, fruits instead of pastry, and finally, plenty of water. Stimulants of all kinds, as well as tobacco, were rigidly forbidden. Courtney watched his men closely to be sure they kept these training rules.

Courtney's special care of his men was always evident in his close attention to the rigging of the boats. He carefully adjusted the rigging to suit the characteristics of the individual members of the crews. He was exceptionally good at this, showing an uncanny sense of how the finest adjustment made a big difference in a man's performance.

Courtney's guardianship of his men was especially pronounced during the trip to Henley, leading to many criticisms of his over-protectiveness. These started on the boat, the *Paris,* going over and continued through the stay in England.

After an exciting send-off in Ithaca, with a parade that included the band, military escort of a platoon of artillery and two companies of infantry, the senior class in caps and gowns, the glee club, almost the entire student body, Ithaca firemen and townspeople, and, in a place of honor, the Henley crew, dressed in their new lounging suits, riding on a float decorated in red and white. A special train took them to New York where they boarded their boat. They left early in June for the races to be held on July 9, 10, and 11.

The *Mail And Express* newspaper sent a reporter with the crew, thus providing "on the spot" accounts of the activities that were sent back to America, arriving about ten days after they were mailed. A long article, headlined "Cornell Men Over The Sea," had a sub-headline, "No 'Good Time' Permitted." Courtney kept a strict eye on the diet and discipline of the crew. The ladies on board wanted to get acquainted with the young men from Cornell, but Courtney's crew was kept to their quarters. They were permitted to jump rope and walk on the deck for exercise, but were not allowed to fraternize with the other 1,178 passengers.

On the ship, they were seated together at a long table in the dining saloon, with Courtney at one end. To illustrate how Courtney watched his men, the reporter related an incident at breakfast the second day out.

> Toward the forward end of the table which the crew occupied there sat a Wall Street man. To make himself agreeable to his neighbor, he passed a menu to Spillman, the nearest oarsman. The starboard optic of Courtney was trained in that direction just then, and he roared out a warning to the sophomore from North Tonawanda. "I'll do the ordering here. No table d'hote meals while I'm around."

The crew's main problem was seasickness, suffered also by their trainer, Courtney, who wanted to go on the ship's log as having escaped seasickness. "All he would admit to at any time was that he had a bad headache," the reporter wrote. He stubbornly stayed on the top deck, maintaining that it was the safest place if the craft should decide to stick her masts in the water. "The stoutest tackle and the most powerful steam winch would have been unable to get the Union Springs carpenter below decks that day," the news account said.

The third day out he turned up for breakfast, but distrust was stamped on his face, and then he hastened away. He did not appear for lunch. A committee was appointed to locate him and finally found him asleep in a stranger's cabin. This led to much banter that evening from University trustee Charles Francis who accompanied the crew. When Courtney complained about the rough voyage and Francis said it wasn't really rough yet, Courtney said, "I have made up my mind what I am going to do when I get to England. If I cannot get a ship that will take me home inside three days, why, I'll remain abroad for good. . . . If I owned this ship I'd fit a centerboard to her keel to keep her from wriggling."

A fire drill resulted in misfortune for the Cornell boats. When the cry "Fire" was heard, there was great hurrying about as the steamship crew prepared lifeboats and cleared passageways. It was just a fire drill, but the excitement was intense. The Cornell men were settling back into their steamer chairs when they heard Courtney, who darted from behind one of the lifeboats and grabbed two sailors who were on the saloon house deck. He pushed one of them up against the middle wall and the other he wanted to throw into the sea. The collegians swarmed to the top of the house and learned that in going to their stations the sailors had trampled on the two new Waters shells that were lying on the house top, one on either side of the funnels. They had done this, notwithstanding the fact that the officers of the vessel were under special instructions from Captain Watkins to prevent any injury to the shells. Courtney, in his excitement, attacked the offenders and "might have given them a severe drubbing had they not sought safety in flight," the reporter wrote.

Courtney incurred the disfavor of the matrons with marriageable daughters on board ship. According the newsman's account, "One lady from Boston, the mother of three angels, sent her maid to Courtney asking if he would present the crew to the young ladies."

Courtney replied that it was impossible for him to oblige. "That's one of the things I draw the line at."

The maid disappeared, but suddenly returned saying that the lady from Boston said, "You are a brute."

"No," said Courtney, slowly. "Just tell the lady that I am their trainer."

That was the starting point of the grand divide between the crew and the belles of the ship. When a man asked Courtney if it was true he would not permit the crew to associate with the young ladies, Courtney said it certainly was. He said he was running "this show" and did not intend to let anyone interfere. He said the friends of Cornell did not subscribe the fund to send these men to England for their health or even for pleasure. "The last crew that represented Cornell in England (a four-oared boat in 1881) had their legs walked off trotting around the deck with the ladies." He intended to get his crew to Henley in the best possible condition. Thus he was "abused by the papas, maligned by the mammas and scolded by the maidens."

Before the crew disembarked at Southampton to board a

special train that was to take them directly to Henley, the American passengers on the ship presented the crew with a resolution, which they all signed and which wished them success in the races for the Grand Challenge Cup. It was a long list of names, filling half a newspaper column.

Although harmony reigned within the crew during the voyage to England, disagreements soon arose when the men reached Henley. The men on the crew squad were: Shape, captain; Hamilton, stroke; Colston, coxswain; Rae, Spillman, Hall, Hager, Louis, Matthews, Dyer, Fennell, Bentley and Freeborn. Also in the group were Francis, a trustee, and Hastings, the commodore, who handled financial matters.

One of the problems arose when some of the crew members would not go along with Courtney's ideas and purposes. He exploded and placed the blame on Shape, the captain, who was supposed to transmit Courtney's wishes to the crew. Courtney told Shape he no longer wanted him as captain, and if he didn't resign, the crew would be without a coach. The crew adviser, Francis, said it was best to remove all obstacles that Courtney thought impeded the progress of the crew. Therefore, Shape resigned and Freeborn was elected. Although Courtney was not exactly pleased with Freeborn, the race was just a week away so no more changes were made.

Another problem was the suggestion to have the men row later in the evening. Daylight breaks at Henley at three o'clock and darkness does not come on much before ten o'clock. It was thought that if the men rowed about 8:30 p.m., or in the cool of the evening, as Trinity Hall and several other crews did, instead of at 5:30 p.m., when the sun is still a great factor, beneficial result would be recorded. Courtney did not endorse this idea. Nor did he approve a suggestion that the men row their practice runs at the same hour, 12:30 p.m., as the rowing of the heats, instead of the usual 10 or 10:30 a.m. His objection was that his men were accustomed to eating dinner at 12:45 p.m. and it would be necessary to change the meal hour if the rowing times were changed. While he saw benefits in having the practice sessions at the time of the heats, he thought the men would suffer a great deal more by a change in their dinner hour.

Courtney became very upset at Hastings for two reasons. The first occurred when Courtney had to practically rebuild one of the Waters shells. Hastings, "who is posing as the society chap of the party because he happens to be the financial man," walked away without leaving Courtney any money to purchase material for alterations. Courtney did not see him in the boathouse for nearly ten days. The repairs had to be made, but Courtney couldn't see the Commodore to tell him what was wanted, "and the result is that he had to run up a bill at Searles's," the reporter wrote. Before the races on July 9, 10, and 11, Courtney almost completely rebuilt the boats.

The second upset happened when Courtney had made all arrangements to start for home on the steamer *New York,* July 20. He had informed Commodore Hastings of his intention at the time that they were on speaking terms. He was, therefore, astonished beyond measure when he learned that Commodore Hastings had changed the entire program and that the crew had been booked to return home by the *St. Louis,* July 27. It was by a mere accident that Courtney learned of the alteration in dates.

He was furious, sought Hastings, but he was not to be found. Courtney tried to book passage himself on July 20, but found all berths filled. So, to rid himself of all the frustration, he went out to Sir John Edwards Moss's preserve and studied pheasant life, the paper said.

Another account of his relaxation activities while in England is recounted in the *Cornell Daily Sun,* telling of his horseback riding. Among the "amusing sights was Courtney astride the horse of James. B. Close, as much at home on a 'gee gee' as a monkey would be sitting stones."

The Henley Regatta, the oldest and most festive in rowing circles, attracted the society crowd as well as the sportsmen. Ladies in lovely, long dresses in pastel shades, wearing broad-brimmed hats and carrying parasols sauntered around the enclosure near the race course. Some of them boarded the pleasure boats on the river to watch the races. Men in stiff, high collars and dapper suits, wore straw hats with narrow brims. The three days of races were a highlight of the social season.

And all in attendance were eager to see the American crew.

The two races entered by the Cornellians had unfortunate results, due to no fault of theirs. The first heat, pitting Cornell against the Leander Boat Club crew over the course of a mile and three eighths, was won by the Cornellians by default, who were criticized loudly in the British press for the circumstances that brought this decision. When both boats lined up at the start, the usual question, "Are You ready?" was asked. No negative replies were given, so the umpire said, "Go." Cornell started and Leander drew away from the post then stopped rowing. The Cornellians soon discovered this, but the umpire waved to them to go ahead. Had the umpire indicated that he wanted them to stop, the Cornell crew would have, the captain, Freeborn, said. The Cornell crew finished the course, with the umpire's boat following it. The Cornellians understood that if they did not row the course they would have been liable to disqualification from entry into any subsequent heat and thereby debarred from further competition for the Grand Challenge Cup. The British claimed Leander did not start and that the Cornellians should have stopped and the race should have been started again.

Unfortunately, no representative of Cornell was on the umpire's boat. Courtney was confined to the crew's quarters because he was sick with a malarial fever, so could not be on hand for this race or the one the next day. He said he got sick after working in the first boathouse they were assigned to which had no floor, just "damp mother earth."

Francis, the University trustee who was there, asked to go on the umpire's boat but was told it was already too full. The only American on board was the reporter for The *Mail And Express.* This reporter blamed his British counterparts on board the umpire's boat for the many false reports "scattered broadcast." He also said the Leander boat showed no indisposition to start before the word "Go." Also, he said the Leander coach blamed the stroke for not continuing despite a possible mistake.

This victory by default was a great disappointment to all

the Americans. Courtney said they went to England to meet the pick of England for the blue ribbons of aquatic England. "We wanted to win on our merits or not at all. We never dreamed of victory by default."

The next day the crew lost to Trinity Hall, a Cambridge University boat, over the same course. Courtney said sickness and the physical condition of several of the men were the main cause of defeat. Fennell, Hager and Rae had been sick, Fennell being the sickest. However, the crews were about even at the milepost. Shortly after that mark, Fennell caught a crab, which knocked the oar out of his hand. Freeborn helped him right himself, but the rest of the crew seemed to slow down, lose its rhythm and Hager missed the water with his oar, almost falling back on Spillman, the two seeming to collapse. They trailed Trinity Hall by a dozen boat lengths.

Courtney said:

> Some people may find fault with me for permitting sick men to row, but I had no other alternative. There were three men—Hager, Fennell and Louis—in bad shape for a fortnight before the regatta. All three had positions on the starboard side of the boat. For a week before the contest the port side pulled the starboard side all around the reach. In taking four stubstitutes aboard, I selected two for the starboard side and two who were accustomed to rowing port sweeps. In substituting Rae for Matthews, I was left with but one starboard substitute. Any old blade will testify to the truth of the statement that it is next to impossible to get an oarsman to ply a sweep on the side opposite to that which he used to. I certainly would have replaced Fennell some time before the race had I had a replacement. When he was well he was one of the strongest men in the boat. . . . The men were not over-trained. They did less work than any of the other crews. I kept them away from the river and the towpath as much as possible after I found that I had malarial fever.

Before Courtney left Henley, a London photographer wrote to him that he had a negative taken at the start of the Leander race, showing both crews in motion. Courtney telegraphed him, asking how much he would sell the plate for and he wired back that he wanted nothing for it, but would give it to Courtney in the interest of fair play.

When he reached Ithaca, Courtney explained that there

was not time for him to get the plate before leaving England. Freeborn was to bring it when he and the crew returned in August. Several members of the crew looked up the photographer in London and sent word to Courtney, who said:

> I received a letter on board when we sailed, signed by Stroke Hall, saying that there were two photographs, one showing Cornell and Leander reaching foward for the stroke and awaiting the word, and the other showing Leander fully ten feet from the starting post. Photographs do not lie, as a rule, and in this particular instance they will right a great wrong that has been done Cornell.

Undoubtedly Courtney hoped these photographs would settle the argument that Leander did not start.

"As to the wisdom of our crew rowing over the course instead of turning back," he said, "had I been there, or had any official representative of Cornell been on the umpire's launch, he or I would certainly have evinced a willingness to have the crew recalled."

When asked if he thought the race against Trinity Hall was decisive, he replied:

> Well, it depends how one looks at it. It certainly decided the fate of Cornell, but to my mind it decided nothing as regards the merits of the two strokes. I still contend that the stroke as rowed by Cornell is the better one for that distance. The race showed nothing, and the question of the superiority of our stroke, coupled with the use of paper boats as against (their) cedar craft, sliding seats set over the keels as against (their) seats in alternate positions; (their) shorter oars with broad blades as against long oars with narrow blades, and patent oarlocks as against the old-fashioned one, is not in the least impaired by the victory of Trinity Hall.

The discussion about the effect of the Henley experience on the Cornell stroke continued for years. Charles V. P. Young writes in *Courtney And Cornell Rowing:*

> His (Courtney's) stroke . . . always included powerful work with the legs and smooth recovery at the end . . . but on comparing the English stroke with the American, he was clever enough to see that while the English back swing was carried to a point where it ceased to be a smooth propelling force, the Americn short swing could be lengthened to

advantage. Combining that modified swing with the leg drive and recovery, he developed a stroke which combined to the nicest degree the maximum of power and speed with the minimum of effort, and which has gradually been adopted by every successful coach in the country.

While the Henley crew was in England, another Cornell eight-oared boat lost to Columbia in the Intercollegiate Rowing Regatta, with Pennsylvania coming in third.

From Courtney and Cornell Rowing

Observation Train on Cayuga Lake

CHAPTER 12

THE MIDDLE YEARS

In 1896 Cornell regained its leadership in rowing competiton. It won the Intercollegiate Rowing Association Regatta at Poughkeepsie, beating Penn, Harvard and Columbia, and setting a new four-mile record of 19 minutes 59 seconds. This victory is noted in Courtney's memorandum of things to be remembered, possibly for a speech, which is in the Cornell University Archives. It merely says:

"1896. Crew won at Pokeepsie. [This was his usual short-cut spelling of the word.] Penn, Harvard, Columbia."

This victory and record made up for the defeats of 1895. Thus, that fall the Cornell Club of New York presented a silver loving cup to Courtney in recognition of his splendid work in developing Cornell crews. In his response at the presentation, Courtney said the credit for the victory should go to the men who plied the oars. Speaking of the crews, he said:

> Cornell has done much for rowing by turning out crews which have been possessed of true sportsmanlike spirit, which have gone in to win, but which have accepted honorable defeat gracefully. I believe they have been thoroughly imbued with the spirit that it is much better to be squarely beaten than to be victorious under any suspicious circumstances, and I am proud to be connected with an institution that develops that kind of men.

As Young points out in his book *Courtney and Cornell Rowing,* this comment is a long step from the professional oarsman who had made an annual circuit of races "pot-hunting," as the racing for prizes was called.

Courtney's speech was probably noted with interest and gratitude by those in the University who opposed hiring former professional athletes as coaches. Courtney's goals in training his men put the emphasis on fair play, not making money from the bets. He never bet on a race himself. He had an aversion to the "crookeds" who flocked to all the professional sporting events and wanted none of that at the University functions. The press, it was said, was responsible to a great degree for the speculation that preceded athletic contests of any kind.

The secretiveness of the professionals was carried over into collegiate rowing, but Courtney is credited with being one of the most influential coaches in doing away with this secretiveness that spawned speculation. At one time, the crews greatly feared being spied upon by their rivals, and the times made in practice were carefully concealed. Often misleading statements gave false impressions about a crew's condition, which gave the bettors more and more fuel. He said that although betting on athletic contests cannot be stopped entirely, it could be lessened if coaches would dispense with the disguises and subterfuges and do everything above board. As the years passed, Courtney saw the tactics become more and more open until he was helping other coaches with rigging of boats and even the coaching itself.

By 1912 Courtney had a generous attitude about helping other crews. That year Stanford University sent a crew east for the intercollegiate regatta at Poughkeepsie without a boat, having ordered one from England which had not arrived. He lent them a shell and even gave them some coaching advice, which was badly needed because their coach also rowed No. 7 and could not see the faults of the crew.

From Courtney and Cornell Rowing

Start of the 1906 Poughkeepsie Race

Parents, alumni and faculty lauded his philosophy that rowing was much more than a good body-builder; it built character. He often said that the long period of training for a place on a crew "offers little to the flashy type of man who must have the prospect of immediate reputation." The long, steady grind, often under disagreeable weather conditions, together with the comradeship of fellow crewmen, was valuable prepartion for life, Courtney thought.

Jacob Gould Schurman, president of Cornell, said, "No sham, no grafter can keep his place for twenty-four hours in Mr. Courtney's boats. I believe that the faculty of this university, and the faculty of every university, has got to learn the lesson which Mr. Courtney is teaching and putting into practice, or else we shall never turn out as distinguished scholars as we do distinguished oarsmen."

In Courtney's memorandum there are five more notations about crews under his care. These notes give us a quick look at what stood out in his mind from the years of that period. The remaining five are:

> 1897. The shortcake crew. Beat Yale, Harvard, Pennsylvania, Columbia at Pokeepsie.

* * *

> 1898. Beat Yale and Harvard at New London. Story of how I was fooled on Cornell's time three days before the race.

* * *

> 1901. Record crew—18.53 1/5 for four miles at Pokeepsie. Story of Duff Robbins and Jakey Smith. Not so much darn Sunday School. Story of the row I took with this crew. Joke on Robbins.

From Courtney and Cornell Rowing

At the Three-Mile Point

1905. Without question the fastest eight-oared crew that ever sat in a boat. Story of the famous 4–mile start.

* * *

1906. Varsity a splendid crew.

The story of the 1897 strawberry shortcake crew is an oft-repeated yarn about the strictness of coach Courtney. When the crews went to Poughkeepsie that year, five members of the varsity ate strawberry shortcake in the hotel dining room. Strawberry shortcake may not be a deadly thing, but one of Courtney's training rules strictly prohibited the eating of any pie or cake during the training period. Courtney caught the shortcake eaters in the midst of their infractions. He looked them over and told them to leave the quarters at once.

"But what will you do for the varsity crew?" one of them asked.

"That's my business," Courtney said. "Go!"

The next day, Courtney had five substitutes in the varsity boat. And to everyone's astonishment they won the varsity race. This suggests that Courtney's thorough training reached all the oarsmen from the very beginning of the season onward.

"I didn't expect them to win," Courtney said, "and I was willing to lose. What happens one year is of little consequence beside what may happen in future years. It is better to have Cornell boys know that they are expected to do what is right than to win a race."

The 1898 crew beat Yale and Harvard but lost the Intercollegiate Rowing Association varsity race to Pennsylvania. In a departure from the usual four-mile Poughkeepsie course, this was over three miles and at Saratoga. This was one of only ten losses for the varsity in the Intercollegiate Rowing Association Regattas during the years 1895 to 1920. Cornell won fourteen of the twenty-four contests.

By that time the organization for the Cornell Navy was running somewhat smoothly. The general policy was determined by the Athletic Council. Details were handled by the Navy Committee, composed of the manager, the captain of the

Cornell Archives

Miss M. M. Crawford takes her first lesson in single sculling from Courtney, who is in the skiff.

crew, and the advisory member, who was chosen by the graduate members of the council. The coach, Courtney, had absolute control of the training and selection of crews, and was responsible for all the property belonging to the crews, including the boathouse, boats and launch. This is not to say that everything always ran smoothly. There were disagreements between Courtney and a graduate manager one year and dissatisfaction with procurement of equipment another, but Courtney stayed on as coach, much to the relief of students and alumni who yearned for Cornell to keep its supremacy on the water.

Although Courtney was not yet 50 in 1898, he had been called "the old man," since the early days of his coaching career, not out of disrespect, but rather from kind regard. The men knew he was strict but fair, they knew he demanded their best, sometimes in a gruff way, but they knew he was kind, too. His relations with his crews stretched from that of an autocratic boss to that of a father-confessor.

On Courtney's birthday, it was customary for the crews, and any former crewmen who were in Ithaca, to gather at his house on Eddy Street to greet him and to share the big birthday cake Mrs. Courtney always baked for the occasion. His "boys" always brought him a remembrance—a book, field glasses or a travelling bag. Then he would tell stories about his days in amateur and professional racing, or he would discuss his escapades as a boy in Union Springs. At these gatherings the "boys" saw the gentle, quietly jovial side of "the old man." Many remembered these talks all their lives, for he was a highly entertaining conversationalist.

Courtney could scold the crews, bluster about things that upset his rowing schedule, such as the debris that floated in the Inlet every spring, getting in the way of the practice sessions, but otherwise he had a pleasant, genial manner. During a race, he would be the quiet man standing off by himself, hard to distinguish from a bystander. Newspapermen who did not know him were surprised when he was pointed out to them; they had expected someone who sought the spotlight, like many of the other coaches who often yelled at their crews from a dock or float.

The 1901 crew that he mentions in his notes, beat Columbia, Wisconsin, Georgetown, Syracuse and Penn in the fastest time recorded between 1895 and 1920 for the four-mile race of the Intercollegiate Rowing Association Regatta at Poughkeepsie—18 minutes 53 1/5 seconds.

This was a welcome victory, ending a losing streak of three years—1898, 1899, and 1900. Young says that it was not because Cornell did not have good crews, but because the winners, Pennsylvania and Wisconsin, were exceptionally fast. Pennsylvania won all three years, with Wisconsin second in 1899 and 1900 and Cornell second in 1898. In spite of the losses, the students and faculty supported Courtney without reservations in the fall of 1900. The college daily paper said he was still the best coach in the country, said they had "unwavering confidence in him" and called for the "right sort of men" to present themselves for the crew. Then followed an appeal to the college community to support the subscription for the Navy. "The Navy belongs to All-Cornell," the paper said. Courtney and the Navy lived up to the expectations in 1901.

Courtney certainly used all his abilities and every possible means he could think of to improve the rowing of his crews. In the late 1890s he had suspected that they were not getting all the power out of the stroke that they should. One day he asked Tom Hall, who had been on the Henley crew and was a graduate student in engineering, if there was a machine that could show just how much power was being applied in the pull of the oar. Hall said there was, borrowed it from the engineering department and hooked it to one of the rowing machines. The device had a recording pen which marked a curve on a sheet of paper as the power it measured increased or fell off.

From At Cornell

Courtney and the coxswains

Courtney said they found that there was a break in the middle of the pull caused by a pause in the body swing at the moment the slide was started. They had been starting the leg drive after beginning the pull with the arms. Courtney's own explanation, as reported by Young, was:

> The curve made by the recording pen went up and then down, and then up again, showing clearly a loss of power just before the middle of the stroke. We experimented and found that we must start the leg drive and the body swing together at the very catch of the oar and carry them through together. In that way we got a single regular curve on the paper, like a wide letter U upside down, showing that we were getting the maximum power in the middle of the stroke, where it ought to be. The stroke as thus modified has been the standard ever since.

Another device Courtney used to help his crews was an invention of his own. He considered proper rigging extremely essential. Since each man in the boat has a different physique—different length in the legs and torso—the same rigging did not suit all of them. Courtney's rigging was individualized by him for each man. About 1900 he developed an apparatus which enabled him to find the exact rigging adapted to each man in the boat, so that when they rowed together they were really in unison, and their blades would catch the water at exactly the same angle.

Beginning in 1899 John Hoyle of Ithaca made all the Cornell shells and oars and helped Courtney with the coaching. Hoyle's traditions were perpetuated for many years after his time. He would not let a boat be launched on Fridays because it would bring bad luck. And when they were launched, it was always stern first because, he said, "They seem to prove better boats if launched stern first."

It was undoubtedly one of these boats that the 1905 crew, mentioned in Courtney's notes, used in its contests. Although it won the Poughkeepsie regatta, its time was slow due to unfavorable water conditions, brought about by the tide which causes rising and falling of the Hudson River at Poughkeepsie. Its time was 20 minutes 29 seconds, much less than the record set by the 1901 crew. But the 1905 boat, which many said at the time was the fastest crew that ever sat in a boat, had previously rowed over the course in 18 minutes 33 seconds and had rowed up-stream in 18 minutes 24½ seconds.

The 1906 crew, which Courtney mentioned in his notes, rowed the Poughkeepsie four-mile course in 19 minutes 36 4/5 seconds. He called it a "splendid crew." It was followed by many more noteworthy crews, two of them given special mention by Young in his book about Courtney and Cornell rowing. They are the 1909 which, with the exception of two men, was the same boat that had rowed as freshman the year before. That year was the third time the Cornell crews made a clean sweep at Poughkeepsie, the freshmen and the four-oared boats winning also. The other years had been 1902 and 1903. The freshmen and four-oared boats set records and the varsity rowed the course in 19 minutes 2 seconds. But, as Young tells the story, it was a very exciting race, with Cornell setting the pace and the other crews constantly challenging the leaders for supremacy. Near the end Columbia was the main challenger, but Cornell's spurt put the boat ahead by a length at the finish line.

The 1911 crew had a boat made by Hoyle that was considerably lighter than the previous boats he made. The original crew, which had started out together as freshmen and had rowed as the varsity shell in 1909 and somewhat the same in 1910, was depleted of its members by death in one family, requirements for engineering camp in June and business matters. So the crew that was the varsity that year was a new set of oarsmen. But they had beaten Harvard, Princeton and Yale by the time they went to Poughkeepsie. This race was won, Young says, not on form and not by precedence early in the race, but by a last desperate effort. Columbia was ahead by a length at the three-mile mark. With yells of "Columbia wins!" in his ears, the Cornell coxswain called for a "twenty," and the crew responded with twenty fast strokes, using all the power in them. The Cornell shell gained a few feet on every pull and was soon even with Columbia. The Columbia bow oarsman fell forward and dropped his oar. The Columbia boat gave a sudden check, and Cornell shot ahead over the finish line. The time was 20 minutes 10 4/5 seconds. It was agreed that Columbia had set too fast a pace.

From At Cornell

Courtney at Poughkeepsie

This led many to comment that no matter how hard the race, the Cornell crews always seemed to have something in reserve. This was believed to be the result of Courtney's strict and sensible training. The Columbia crew had not had that extra reserve when needed.

Courtney did not believe in long distance races, saying, "I don't believe in a four-mile race. I never did, and I am unalterably opposed to it for the reason that the average student can't give the necessary time from his university work to make proper preparation for it . . . In rowing, as in any form of exercise, there must be a moderate beginning with a gradually increasing amount of work."

He saw no need to have men injured by the extra strain of the longer races, which required a longer time for them to recover. Constant and expert supervision was the only ways to guard against any injury. The shorter distance would decrease the chances for any physical harm. And he was sure that his crews would make "just as serious an affair of the three-mile race as the four," and would take just as long to train.

The men in the Cornell crews at this period, beginning in the early 1900s, undoubtedly benefited from Courtney's use of photography. His eagle eye was sharp in detecting flaws in his crews, but photographs gave him a chance to show the boys just what was the matter. He was an expert amateur photographer, and kept a large camera with him on board the coach's launch. In the evenings at home he studied the pictures and made notes about what corrections were needed. Many of these photographs and notes regarding the positions of all the crews, in practice sessions and in races, are in the Cornell University Archives.

Courtney studied rowing as other men study a science. His meticulous attention to every detail was equalled only by his devotion to his men and the sport.

CHAPTER 13

THE COURTNEY STROKE

Although Courtney sometimes claimed there was no such thing as "a Courtney stroke"—that it was just a matter of pulling hard and getting there first, other people quickly realized that the young oarsman from Union Springs had a way of rowing that assured him victory. Throughout the years, it was said to be the same stroke he developed in 1873 when he won his first big contest at Saratoga.

Charles W. Francis, champion single sculler from Cornell and later University trustee and United States diplomat, said this stroke was the same one, with some modifications, that Courtney taught him and which enabled him to win the intercollegiate championship race in 1876 at Saratoga.

One of the first modifications that Courtney made to "what came naturally" was to maintain a straight back. He noticed the advantage of a straight back when he saw Harry Coulter row at Buffalo in 1870.

Perhaps the best description of the stroke is found in Young's book *Courtney and Cornell Rowing,* and is said to be Courtney's explanation in his own words, found on pages 90, 91 and 92 of the book, as follows:

> First of all, I regard it as essential to keep the oars in the water the longest possible time, and in the air the shortest possible time. The blades should hold onto the water as long as possible, but never beyond the point when, in so doing, power is sacrificed. When the stroke is finished, the hands should be dropped sharply in the lap, the blades of the oars coming clearly out of the water at right angles to it, and the arms shot forward as quickly as possible for another stroke. The slide on the recovery should be started at first rapidly, but gradually slowed up before the finish in order not to have the weight of the oarsman brought up too suddenly on the stretcher,

which would as a matter of course retard the boat.

Too much attention cannot be paid to the leg work. The legs are, of course, the strongest part of the body; and, to my way of thinking, they should, therefore, be required to do the greatest amount of work in rowing. An oarsman should not try to keep the knees tight together, for by so doing he occupies a cramped position and is physically handicapped at just the time when the most work is demanded of him. On the other hand, he should not open his legs too wide, for he is then pulling around a corner. Unless the knees are in an easy position, the muscles are strained and considerable power is lost.

The back should be straight, as the lungs are then enabled to do their work more easily and satisfactoriy, and there is no unnecessary strain upon the abdominal muscles. The bend should be at the hips, and with no kink in the back. Another point which cannot be too closely followed is to keep the arms perfectly straight until the shoulders have gone back as far as it is intended they should go. The shoulders should never go back so far that it is an effort to bring them to the perpendicular. While I am firmly impressed with the belief that a straight back is desirable in an oarsman, it must be admitted that it is not absolutely demanded of

Cornell Archives

This is the measuring machine that Courtney used to check the measurements of the men so he could adapt the rigging to each oarsman.

a fast sculler, for there are many living examples to the contrary.

At the catch, the blade should not be dropped in at a perfect right angle, but should be inclined just a trifle, so that it will enter the water easily and cleanly, scoop fashion. The blade should strike the water very sharply, and no time should be wasted before applying the power to the stroke. All there is to this part of the stroke is to get the blade into the water cleanly, and to get it in without wasting time. It should always be covered fully, however, and kept covered. Right here I would remark about a great fault with many oarsmen, that the blade should not be sunk too deep in the water, but it should always be covered. The stroke can be rowed so that to a casual observer it appears as if the oarsman's blade were covered, while in reality it is only the pressure of the water against the blade forcing itself against it and apparently covering it. Great care should be taken to have the blade as close to the water as possible before the catch, in order to avoid 'clipping,' which is the fault of many an oarsman who in other respects does fairly well.

Cornell Archives

The 1906 crew in front of the boathouse that was relatively new then.

> Summed up, then, the oarsman should have his oar in the water as long as possible, and the least possible time in the air. He should never overreach, and should be equally careful to avoid going back too far at the end of the stroke. He should catch the water firmly with the blades slightly inclined in (a difficult thing to teach a crew, however), and should pull the stroke through from beginning to end, bringing the blades cleanly out of the water at right angles and with a snap. Don't hang when the stroke is finished, but let the hands drop and shoot the arms forward like lightning, the slide following at first quickly but gradually decreasing in speed. Don't lose any time in dropping the blades into the water when they are back in position for the catch. Pull with straight arms until the shoulders are back to the farthest point it is intended to carry them. Never buckle and slide up to meet the handles of the oars. Avoid dropping the shoulders and kinking the back. Bend from the hips. On the recovery, of course, keep the blades as close to the water as practicable without striking the surface. But above all else, remember that if you desire to make your boat go fast, you have got to pull like the devil, and never for a moment forget the fact that the shortest distance between two points is a straight line.

The late George S. Kephart, Cornell Class of 1917, who was a coxswain under Courtney, read the above description of the stroke and had some questions about it, as he remembered it. He sent his comments to the late John Collyer, Class of 1917 and an accomplished oarsman under Courtney, asking for verification of his comments. Kephart sent copies of his comments and correspondence to the author. Kephart's comments follow:

> In the winter months I frequently went up to the crew room, during off hours, to work out on a rowing machine and try to get the feel of the stroke. If there were no oarsmen practicing at the time, Mr. Courtney often encouraged me with a bit of personal coaching. But after 60 years my recollections of the stroke may easily be distorted. There is also a possibility, however, that Courtney was misquoted in the above excerpt from *Courtney And Cornell Rowing.*
>
> I hope someone will set my thinking straight, by verifying the quoted description or agreeing with my recollections. [As to] . . . "keep the arms perfectly straight until the shoulders have gone as far back as it is intended they should go" . . . and similar statements [in the last paragraph]. It is my recollection that power of legs, back and arms was used; and therefore, that the arms were flexed to

> bring the oar up to the body [not the body up to the oar]. It is also my recollection that the three actions were completed simultaneously. If the arms were kept straight until the shoulder swing [and leg drive?] were completed, the arm flexing would be the last, and weakest part of the stroke. Would it not also increase the tendency to buckle or slide up to meet the oar instead of using the arm power to pull the oar back to the body?
>
> "At the catch, the blade . . . should be inclined just a trifle." It is my recollection that the blade entered the water vertically, although I can understand that a slight inclination could make for a clean entry. But if the blade should remain inclined throughout the stroke, would it not tend to dig the blade even deeper, and also tend to pull the boat down into the water, instead of lifting it out? If inclined at the start, was the blade eventually brought to the vertical and, if so, at what point in the stroke?"

Collyer wrote back, "All you said in your letter regarding the techniques used by Mr. Courtney are valid."

Kephart also sent the author a copy of a letter he wrote to some friends, which contained reminiscences of his days as coxswain of the crew. Kephart wrote:

> As to the Courtney stroke, here are some recollections which, over a span of more than 65 years, may have strayed from fact. All newcomers to the boathouse, whether or not with previous rowing experience, were lined up in front of Johnny Hoyle [who assisted Courtney in coaching]. He would then demonstrate the basic principles of the stroke by likening it to the lifting of a heavy object. He would squat down to start the lift, instead of merely bending at the waist, thus being roughly in the desired position of an oarsman at the start of the stroke. Then his leg push-up,

Courtney took many pictures, which he showed to the men and pointed out flaws in their form.

Cornell Archives

back bend and (I beleive) arm flexing would all start together in lifting the weight. These three actions continued and ended together. The finish of the weight lift and the finish of the stroke would be at different points, and other slight differences would become evident as the oarsman's instruction progressed. But the point was—all muscles of the body working in harmony to develop the greatest power and the least likelihood of strain to any muscles.

Hoyle also said that the hands, and therefore the oar blade, should describe rectangles. Vertical drop into the water, straight-line pull through the water, vertical lift from the water and parallel straight-line return to the starting point. I believe my memory is correct that Courtney stressed the obvious—that, except when exerting force on the oar during the stroke, the oarsman's vital function is to disturb the forward motion of the shell as little as possible. Clean entry and exit of the oar blade, maintaining an even keel, properly feathered oar, no kick against the foot rest until and as the blade re-enters the water, no rushing of the seat or lunging of the body on the recovery, which would impede the run of the boat, etc.

One item, as I remember it, was distinctly different from the present stroke (as I understand it). Courtney wanted the oar feathered and hands and slide started on the recovery rapidly and

Cornell Archives

This is an example of Courtney's photography of a crew practicing.

> smoothly, with no pause at the end of the stroke. The recovery was then continued at an even pace, with no hurry up at the end. To him, time lost before starting the recovery means that the whole recovery process thereafter must be speeded up to make up for that pause. And this increased speed and force of eight husky men traveling in a direction opposite to that of the shell has a damping effect upon the shell's run just at the time when the run itself is fading.
>
> Of course, today's crews are preparing for the sprints, rather than the four-mile and other non-sprint distances. So this suggests modifications. And it would be strange indeed if accumulated experience over many years since Courtney used his stroke had not developed some improvements.

Kephart generously shared some of his experiences as a coxswain under Courtney, but that is another chapter.

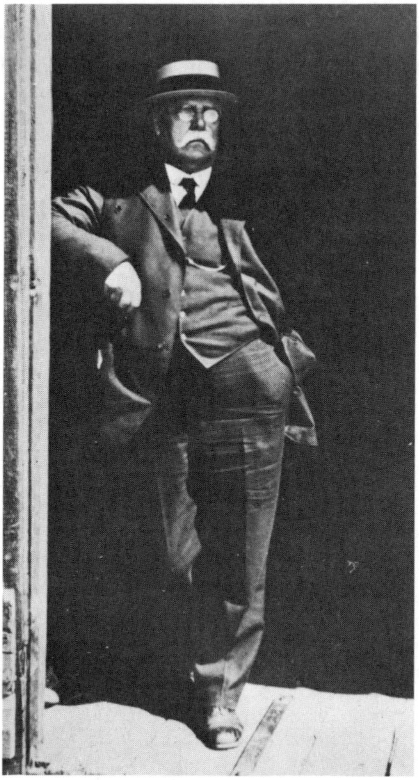

Cayuga County Historical Society

Courtney in his later years, watching his crews from a doorway at the boathouse.

CHAPTER 14

THE LATER YEARS

The Courtneys did not have any children of their own, but raised his four nephews after the death of his brother John, the boys' father, in 1908. John's wife Bessie died in 1906. The nephews were William F., Edwin Claire, J. Howard and Charles E., 2nd. They ranged in age from 12 to 20 at the time of their father's death. And then, of course, the Courtneys' "boys," the crews, were always considered "family."

Courtney's wife, Della, who is listed on official documents as Sarah D. Courtney, took a motherly interest in the crews. When they went to Poughkeepsie, she went ahead of time to inspect their quarters, which often in the later years were at "The Oaks" at Highland across the river from Poughkeepsie. In 1914 she took particular pains to be sure everthing was disinfected, because there was a scarlet fever epidemic in the city. She engaged chemists to analyze the water, and after the men arrived she carefully supervised the preparation of their food. Infections causing painful boils were common if living quarters were not clean. So, as she did every year, she made sure the crews' quarters were spotlessly clean. The result was that Cornell crews had the least absences due to infections of any of the crews. "Physicians can make my men well if they become ill, but Mrs. Courtney beats them to it. She doesn't let the boys get ill," Courtney told the Poughkeepsie newspaper.

That year Cornell won the freshman and junior varsity races, but the varsity lost to Columbia at Poughkeepsie. But none of the boys caught scarlet fever, thanks to Mrs. Courtney's efforts.

In the Courtney files at the Cornell University Archives there are notebooks containing records of some of the family's

Cornell Archives

Mrs. Della (Sarah D.) Courtney, wife of the coach, who considered all the crews "her boys."

expenses for the nephews, giving their ages and sizes and various needs. There is the record of the purchase of a 45 horsepower Berkshire auto and all its equipment for $800 in 1908. Courtney wrote that the "machine is Mrs. C.'s because it was bought with her money from Charles R. Robinson. Had first ride in it on Dec. 13. John Egbert and Robinson ran it."

Among Courtney's papers there are many programs from alumni gatherings that honored him, such as those of the Classes of 1904, 1909, 1912 and 1915.

He spoke to numerous alumni groups, including three in 1914. These were in St. Louis, Milwaukee and Chicago. At all of them he used the topic, "Too Much Athletics At Cornell." His chief concern was that so many athletes were on probation. His explanation was that the students were spending too much time on athletics. He asked, "Are our boys willfully neglecting their university work, or are the coaches demanding and taking more of the boys' time than they can afford to give to athletics and at the same time do their university work?"

He had discussed the problem with the other coaches and with some of the students, including football players, who said their athletic pursuits made them so tired they could not study. He objected to out-of-town athletic events being scheduled during the week, so that students missed classes. He urged more emphasis on scholarship, saying that the manufacturing concerns were not looking for fine athletes but for men who came to the University to get an education. He objected to graduate managers who had considerable control over the athletic teams' finances, and suggested the athletics be run more efficiently.

Courtney lamented that the scholastic standing of his crews was going down. He had always been proud that they kept up in their university work. He had stressed to them that the university work was the most important part of their college lives, and now there were so many races they could not keep up their studies.

Courtney had often said that he wished he had more education. Perhaps this shortcoming of his own was behind his viewpoint as expressed in these speeches. The faculty and administration should have felt encouraged that the University's leading coach was urging a sensible approach to athletics.

Courtney's papers abound with records of crews. Nearly every daily notation tells what the weather was that day—even when it was too bad for the crews to go on the water. Always there is marked in bold print or underlined type the day the crews went on the water for the first time each season.

Courtney had a reputation for wanting to speed up the breaking of the ice on the Inlet so the crews could practice as early as possible in the spring. He even took unusual means to assure the earliest possible practice date. Romeyn Berry, in his

Cornell Archives

The men on a float are breaking up the ice in front of the boathouse in the spring. Courtney did everything possible to rid the Inlet of ice as early as possible so the crews could practice on water.

book, *Behind The Ivy*, describes Courtney's annual efforts to get the ice out of the Inlet. He resorted to dynamite, clearly against the city and county codes. No one objected because, after three decades of leading winning Cornell crews, there was a wall of public opinion around Mr. Courtney "which left him free to dynamite ice."

The boathouse handyman, Ben Gifford, was sent to the athletic office every few days with an order for supplies for the crews—varnish, oil, soap. According to Berry, when the blasting season drew near, usually in March, Gifford would whisper something to the secretary, and soon there would be appear a cash voucher for $30 charged to "rowing miscellaneous."

That was the entire transaction. But a week later, Gifford would appear with a large package of fish ready for the pan, for the secretary and another for the official at the athletic office. Berry suspected that the game warden and chief of police received similar gifts from the rowing establishment.

Berry tells another anecdote about Courtney and the faculty. The latter was always spoiling Courtney's crews by putting some of the men on probation. Courtney took drastic steps. He ordered the *Cornell Sun* to stop its custom of publishing the boatings of the day before. Rowing news quietly dropped from the paper. He proudly explained to the athletic office that there would "be no more leaks from the boathouse." Then he roared triumphantly, "Now, how are the faculty going to bust out the oarsmen, if they don't know who the oarsmen are?"

In 1915, on the way to Poughkeepsie, Courtney was thrown against a berth and fractured his skull when the train stopped suddenly. Although he tried to resume his coaching, his recovery was slow. In 1916 he said he would step down for a while, just being on hand to give advice to John Hoyle, who with John Collyer, carried the load of the coaching work. Collyer had stroked the varsity in 1915 that won the Poughkeepsie race.

Diaries and letters that George Kephart, a coxswain under Courtney, kept indicate that the Spring Day race of 1916 may have been Courtney's last great effort.

Kephart's letter to Collyer, a copy of which Kephart sent to the author, refers to an article in the *Cornell Alumni News* of February 1977 about the filming of the 1916 Spring Day events, including the race. Kephart was the Cornell varsity coxswain. Excerpts follow:

> Would you agree that the race, while exciting, also marked an unhappy milestone in the history of intercollegiate crew racing? Was it not the last time that Courtney called into play the full knowledge, skill and genius that had made him the "Grand Old Man" among crew coaches?
>
> The makeup of the Spring Day crew hints of the near miracle he performed. If my memory is correct, only three of the nine men had ever before been in an intercollegiate race. . . . Until five weeks before the race, the coxswain, and perhaps one or two others, had never sat in a racing shell. Their experience was with the eight-oared gigs, the heavier boats, used by the intercollege crews.
>
> I have no doubt that, for every a man in the final crew, there was an equally competent or superior oarsman among the others who were working out at the time. It was certainly true among the coxswains.
>
> But I have little doubt that Courtney brought together, for that Spring Day race, the best available balance of capabilities—the nine men who worked best together, and developed the best total

Cornell Archives

This is the 1916 crew with George S. Kephart as coxswain. Others in the crew are: bow, J. C. Othus; No. 2, W. Calder; No. 3, T. H. Farnsworth; No. 4, L. D. Kingsland; No. 5, B. Kirkland; No. 6, W. F. Courtney; No. 7, W. G. Cowan; stroke, A. Aloe.

power for a two-mile race. Being an immobile coxswain in the boat, I could generally sense the improvement as favorable changes were made—the increase in power, in uniform respose to changes in pace, in maintained even keel, in clean run without checking, and in the fact that virtually no steering became necessary, except to compensate for wind and wave.

I believe each man realized that he could put forth his best effort because his outrigger and footrest had been adjusted to his special needs by Courtney himself. And I imagine each of the others also received some of Courtney's individually applied psychology, of mixed praise and censure. And the "leaked" reports of time trials.

I wonder if Courtney didn't deliberately select an inexperienced crew for the race. Only two among us had earned as much as a J. V. insignia; another his Frosh numerals. And, with one exception, we were Juniors and Seniors. Suddenly, there was held before us the chance to reach the unreachable goal of a Varsity "C" or a J.V. insignia. The will to win was with us abundantly.

I seem to recall that morale was low in the early days of spring practice, because of Courtney's failing health. His suddenly renewed vitality, as he developed the Spring Day crew, was a needed tonic for the entire squad. Every one at the boathouse seemed to be solidly behind us as we went into final practice for that race. After the race, Courtney seemed to yield again to the infirmities, and never regained his spirit.

Kephart kept a diary during that period and sent the author a copy of the entries beginning on March 27, 1916 and ending May 31. Some of them follow:

March 27—Guess I'll go out for Ag. crew again this year. (I had gained weight, and there seemed little chance that I could get down to coxie weight.)

March 30—Crews went on water for first time this spring.

April 17—Intercollege crew started fairly well now. I weighed 124 lbs. yesterday.

April 24—Si Seymour called up and said I am wanted to coxie 4th varsity. Just as we were getting Ag. crew started!

April 26—Went out with the 4th varsity again. We had a shell (instead of a gig) but stayed on the Inlet (instead of going on the lake). This is the third time that I have ever been in a shell.

Then for the next two weeks, Courtney changed and rechanged the combinations in the boat. On May 1 Kephart wrote that they were now the 3rd varsity.

May 4—Same bunch tonight except Cowan for Galbraith. I can get down to 115—there are three others that can get down to 105.

May 10—(After many more changes in the boat.) Awfully rough on the lake. The waves broke over the outriggers. The "Old Man" asked me how much I weighed. I told him 120, and he said, "I wish you weighed 110."

May 12—I got my death sentence so far as any insignia goes. The "Old Man" called me in and wanted to know if I could still get on the Ag. crew. He said he wished I could get down to 110, but he didn't want me to try, and hurt myself. I told him I could get down to 115 all right without any harm, but he didn't believe me.

May 13—Who said you should quit? Tonight the "Old Man" said, "Do you think you can get down to 115?" I said, "I know I can." Whereupon he replied, "Well, suppose you try." Later he said, "I wouldn't try to get down yet. You know it's about five weeks yet to Poughkeepsie."

Courtney handed out acid as well as sweet stuff. Returning to the boathouse on another evening, rather cocky after we had won a race (practice), I brought the shell up to the float too fast and too close. Courtney said, for all to hear, "The next time you do that, you go up the hill."

Cornell Archives

Courtney, left, and John Hoyle in the launch.

Cornell Archives

Courtney in the launch, holding his megaphone, 1918.

May 18—Varsity and Frosh left for Cambridge. We went out in the new 1916 shell . . . Courtney did not go to Cambridge. Gave us special training while the others were away.

May 21—Crew got back today. Started training down a little, in case anything should happen.

May 23—Got our old bunch back again tonight. We won by 2 lengths in a 2-mile (practice) race. Weighed 118. Last night we did the 1 5/16 miles in 6 minutes 23 seconds. The "Old Man" said we rowed the half mile faster than he had ever seen it rowed except once before.

May 24—I am going in the Varsity race against Princeton and Yale. For the first time I'll be representing the University. Princeton has a wonderful crew, and I don't know what Yale can do.

May 25—Princeton came in today. They certainly are a wonderful crew.

May 26—Yale came today. They use the English stroke and thole pins.

May 27—We won! It was sure some race. . . . The Princeton fellows are a mighty fine bunch. Just like Cornellians. I can't say as much for Yale.

[This race was such a close one between Cornell and Princeton, Yale having fallen far behind, that the Princeton students refused to beleive that they lost until they saw the film of the race made by the Cornell photographers.]

May 31—Collyer came before I was up this morning and told me to be ready to go to Poughkeepsie on Sunday. The thing I have been working for ever since I entered college.

Collyer wrote to Kephart with recollections of the Poughkeepsie race, which Cornell lost to Syracuse, as follows:

I do recall that the four-mile race was rowed in fairly rough water. You may recall that just before we left the float, Mr. Courtney sent a message that my outrigger should be raised. It was on our way to the starting mark that I knew the outrigger had been lowered rather than raised, making it difficult for me to feather properly.

Our crew was asked to stop a few minutes later and we were told that a man in the Syracuse crew had lost control of his oar within the time allowed for requesting a new start.

You may recall that our next start was not nearly so favorable as the first and also that the wind had freshened, making it difficult for me to function properly with the lowered outrigger. The four-mile race was a close one right to the finish line.

A few days later, after this race, I was asked to succeed Mr. Courtney as head coach on his recommendation. Mr. Courtney took over his old job in 1918.

Other miscellaneous notes from Kephart's diaries include the story, unconfirmed, he said, that Courtney agreed to coach the women's crews. He resigned, one day abruptly and red-faced, after shouting to one of the girls, "You're shooting out your tail too fast."

Kephart helped to cox the women's crews, which at that time rowed on Beebe Lake on the campus. The seniors

Cornell Archives

This is the 1918 crew with Charles (Mike) Hendrie as coxswain. Others in the crew are: bow, Wipperman; No. 2, Knight; No. 3, Egbert; No. 4, Davenport; No. 5, Stott; No. 6, E. B. Smith; No. 7, Hall; stroke, Swartz.

presented him a knife for a watch chain in appreciation of his work for them.

Kephart wrote to the author, "I doubt that any other professional coach received and earned such respect and admiration from his pupils."

Charles F. Hendrie, "Mike" of the Cornell Class of 1919, sent the author some recollections of his years as a coxswain, as follows:

> In November [1917] Courtney was again at the boathouse watching three varsity and four freshman combinations work out on the gigs, which were used in the spring until the ice had left the Inlet. When we finally were allowed into the more fragile shells, I recall one instance of a competing cox deciding to steer his crew around the island instead of directly into the main Inlet. Unfortuneatley, it encountered a thin sheet of skim ice which ripped a hole in the bottom of that expensive shell. After retrieving the shell to dry land and returning to the boathouse, the cox lost no time in gathering up his clothes and rushing up the hill to escape the "Old Man's" censure.
>
> I have a mental picture of the "Old Man" standing in one of the open doors on the second floor of the boathouse, with his megaphone, as the crews left the float, and later in his launch, on the Inlet of the lake, encouraging each oarsman or correcting faulty stroking. He was still not his old self, however, and concentrated on coaching the Varsity and J.V., leaving the Frosh to his assistant, John Hoyle.

Hendrie was among the many students who served in the armed forces during the next two years. During that time, athletics were only held between the colleges at the University.

Hendrie said, "He insisted on adherence to his rules of training and morality, for which we all admired him."

As the dean of university rowing coaches, Courtney was often asked his opinion on matters related to his field. In January 1917 his stand against the four-mile race brought comments from Harvard and Yale, both having proposed eliminating the four-mile race earlier. His reputation as an eminent rowing coach carried a great deal of weight, so the press forecast a serious discussion about reducing the length of the Poughkeepsie race course.

Later the same year, he was asked about the use of a standard shell, as proposed by Syracuse. He favored the idea but promptly cited the disadvantage, saying he thought a standard shell would discourage experimentation with shells and rigging.

In July 1920, Courtney and his wife were at the cottage of a friend, called "The Castle," near Union Springs for a vacation. He went out in his boat in the morning, hoping to catch some fish for guests who were expected later in the day. About 11:30 in the morning, he returned to the shore, left his boat without removing the oars from their locks and drew the craft up on shore. This negligence was uncharacteristic of the man.

When he hurried into the house, his wife noticed that his face was flushed. He complained of being ill and went upstairs. She immediately called the doctor, but Courtney was dead from apoplexy before the physician arrived.

Thousands mourned him and sent condolences to his widow and to the University. The funeral service was held at his home at 218 Eddy Street, Ithaca, and he was buried in Lake View cemetery there.

His old friend, William Hoagland, the champion heel and toe walker and now a Game Protector, had expected to go fishing with Courtney that weekend and was greatly saddened by the sudden death of his friend. Expressions of grief came from rowing coaches all over the world, and the newspapers were lavish in their eulogies. He was called the genius of American rowing, a coach without peer, an unrivaled teacher, the "Grand Old Man of rowing" and the greatest oarsmen in America.

Many years later, Morris Bishop in his book, *A History of Cornell,* refers to the seven clean sweeps that Courtney's crews made in the Intercollegiate Regattas, then adds that this is the power of a great coach, which "is not too much to call genius."

And again, in the same book, Bishop says that after Courtney's death, when other crew coaches were sought, "no comparable genius could be found, since none existed."

Today, in the crew room in Teagle Hall, a large picture of

Photo by the author

This picture shows the seat in a Courtney shell that hangs on the wall in the crew room today in Teagle Hall at Cornell University.

Courtney in his later years looks down on the Cornell crews practicing in the tanks, the equipment he greatly coveted after he heard Harvard and Yale had them. Beside the picture is the jeweled badge he won at the 1876 International Regatta in Philadelphia, when he became the amateur single sculling champion. Above this display is one of his shells, built about 1880 and donated by W. Frederick Davis, Class of 1921, of Auburn, and his brother Jerry R. Davis who lived in the Courtney home in Union Springs. With the display is Courtney's statement, imparting inspiration to today's crews at Cornell:

> Some day, fellows, when I am big enough, strong enough and know enough, I am going to row a boat on these waters, row to beat any man living; and when I have done that, I am going to train boys to row so that those I teach will beat all others. . . .
>
> Charles Edward Courtney
> 1849–1920
> Master Oarsman and Champion Coach

And so Courtney's spirit reigns today. Cornellians through the years, whether they knew him or not, will always think of him with respect and affection as "Pop" Courtney or the "Old Man," and agree that he was a master oarsman and champion coach.

Photos by the author

The Courtney homestead in Union Springs, owned today by the Gibbs family, is a historic landmark. The marker cites Courtney's achievements.

Cornell Archives

Charles E. Courtney

PRINCIPAL SOURCES

Prologue

Ithaca Journal, July 1950.

Chapter 1

Anthony, Nellie Larmon, *Master Coach,* (privately published, no date), Part I.

Hewett, Waterman Thomas, *Cornell University, A History* (Ithaca: Cornell University Press, 1905), Vol. III: 208–215.

Young, Charles Van Patten, *Courtney And Cornell Rowing* (Ithaca: Cornell University Press, 1923), 11–14.

Chapter 2

Bicentennial Committee History Of Springport And Union Springs, New York (Ovid: W. E. Morrison & Co., 1976), 25, 28, 40–51, 90, 113, 117.

Encyclopedia Americana (New York, Chicago, Washington, D.C.,1957), Vol. XXIII: 729–731.

Hewett, Waterman Thomas, *Cornell University, A History,* Vol. III: 215–219.

Stroke, Elliott G., *History of Cayuga County, New York* (Syracuse: D. Mason & Co, 1879; reprinted Interlaken: Heart of the Lakes Publishing, 1980), 375, 376.

Young, Charles Van Patten, *Courtney And Cornell Rowing,* 20–23.

Chapter 3

Ithaca Journal, 1873: September 9, 12, 13, 15; 1874: September 10, 11, 12; 1875: June 1, August 24, 25, 26 and September 4, 6, 9, 10, 20, 21, 22.

Chapter 4

Auburn Daily Advertiser 1877: July 24.

History of Centennial Exhibition, 1876 (Philadelphia, no publication date), 673–689.

Chapter 5

Auburn Daily Advertiser, 1877: July 17, 18, 19, 24.
Hewett, Waterman Thomas, *Cornell University, A History,*), Vol. III: 219, 220.
Ithaca Journal, 1877: July 14.
New York Times, 1877: July 18.

Chapter 6

Anthony, Nellie Larmon, *Master Coach,* Part II.
Ithaca Journal, 1877: October 18.

Chapter 7

Hewett, Waterman Thomas, *Cornell University, A History,* Vol. III: 220.
Ontario History, (December 1974), Vol. LXVII: 244.
Police Gazette, (New York, 1880), *Edward Hanlan,* 9, 10.

Chapter 8

This chapter appeared in similar form in:
The Post-Journal, Jamestown, N.Y., October 18, 1969
Rowing U.S.A., Dec. 1982–Jan. 1983, Feb.–Mar. 1983.
Cornell Alumni News, June 1983.
The Post-Journal, September 14, 1985.
Auburn Daily Advertiser, 1879: October 14, 16, 17, 18, 21, 23, 25.
Hewett, Waterman Thomas, *Cornell University, A History,,* Vol. III: 220, 221.
The Daily Journal, 1879: September, October; 1880: May, June.

Chapter 9

Cornell University, Department of Manuscripts and Archives, Charles E. Courtney Papers, No. 40/1/142 and 40/1/924.
Young, Charles Van Patten, *Courtney And Cornell Rowing:* 26.

Chapter 10

Anthony, Nellie Larmon, *Master Coach,* Part II.
Bishop, Morris, *A History Of Cornell* (Ithaca: Cornell University Press, 1962), 248, 297.
Charles E. Courtney Papers, 40/1/142.
Hewett, Waterman Thomas, *Cornell University, A History,* Vol III: 226, 233–235.
Young, Charles Van Patten, *Courtney And Cornell Rowing:* 19, 20, 27–29, 31–39, 57, 63.

Chapter 11

Charles E. Courtney Papers, 40/1/7229.
Mail And Express, 1895: June 15, July 2, 5, 10.
Young, Charles Van Patten, *Courtney And Cornell Rowing:* 43, 47.

Chapter 12

Charles E. Courtney Papers, 40/1/7229.
Hewett, Waterman Thomas, *Cornell University, A History,* Vol. III: 224, 226, 227, 237.
Troy Daily Times, 1898: special edition.
Young, Charles Van Patten, *Courtney And Cornell Rowing,* 46, 53–61, 69–77.

Chapter 13

Hewett, Waterman Thomas, *Cornell University, A History:* 229, 230.
Kephart, George S., private papers and correspondence 1977.
Young, Charles Van Patten, *Courtney And Cornell Rowing:* 90–96.

Chapter 14

Berry, Romeyn, *Behind The Ivy* (Binghamton, 1950), 174, 175.
Cornell Alumni News, (Ithaca: Cornell University Alumni Assn.), 1914, February 1977.
Charles E. Courtney Papers, 40/1/142 and 40/1/924.
Hendrie, Charles F., private papers and correspondence.
Kephart, George S., private papers and correspondence.

ABOUT THE AUTHOR

Margaret K. Look, a graduate of The Ellis School in Pittsbrugh, Pennsylvania and Cornell University, Class of 1937, lived in Jamestown, New York for many years where she worked for the daily newspaper, the *Post-Journal,* serving as news editor for eight years. Since moving to Powell, Wyoming in 1977, she has worked for the *Powell Tribune* and as a free lance writer with articles appearing in national and regional magazines and a short story in an anthology of fiction by Wyoming writers. She won the 1986 national fiction contest sponsored by the American Mothers, Inc. This is her third book.

Her first book, *At Home On The Workhouse Farm,* describes her family's life on the Allegheny County Workhouse Farm near Pittsburgh, where her father was farm manager for many years.

Her second book, *At Home In Pittsburgh,* describes her early childhood in that city in the 1920s, bringing in many of the customs and attitudes of that era.

Mrs. Look has a son and a daughter, and three grandchildren. Her husband, Travis, is a retired attorney.